O9-ABI-747

World Book's

SCIENCE
& NATURE
GUIDES

RESOURCES &
CUMULATIVE
INDEX

World Book, Inc.
a Scott Fetzer company
Chicago

World Book, Inc.
233 North Michigan Avenue
Chicago, IL 60601 USA

For information about other World Book publications, visit our Web site **http://www.worldbook.com,** or call **1-800-WORLDBK (967-5325).** For information about sales to schools and libraries, call **1-800-975-3250 (United States); 1-800-837-5365 (Canada).**

ISBN 0-7166-4216-6   ISBN 0-7166-4208-5 (set)

For World Book:
General Managing Editor: Paul A. Kobasa
Editorial: Shawn Brennan, Maureen Liebenson,
    Christine Sullivan
Research: Madolynn Cronk, Lynn Durbin, Cheryl Graham,
    Karen McCormack, Loranne Shields, Hilary Zawidowski
Librarian: Jon Fjortoft
Permissions: Janet Peterson
Graphics and Design: Sandra Dyrlund, Anne Fritzinger
Indexing: Aamir Burki, David Pofelski
Pre-press and Manufacturing: Carma Fazio, Steve Hueppchen,
    Jared Svoboda, Madelyn Underwood
Text Processing: Curley Hunter, Gwendolyn Johnson
Proofreading: Anne Dillon

Printed in China
1 2 3 4 5 6 7 8 9 10 09 08 07 06 05 04

Contents

Time Scale of Earth's History

Time divisions			Years spanned by time division	What life was like during time division
Cenozoic Era	Quaternary Period	Holocene Epoch	11½ thousand years ago to present day	Humans hunted and tamed animals and developed agriculture. Humans also learned to use metals, coal, oil, gas, and other natural resources.
		Pleistocene Epoch	2 million to 11½ thousand years ago	Modern humans appeared. Mammoths, woolly rhinoceroses, and other large mammals were common, but then died out.
	Tertiary Period	Pliocene Epoch	5 million to 2 million years ago	Modern-type sea life became common. Birds and mammals spread throughout the world. Humanlike creatures appeared.
		Miocene Epoch	24 million to 5 million years ago	Apes were common in Asia and Africa. Other animals included bats, monkeys, whales, bears, and raccoons. Modern-type flowering plants became common.
		Oligocene Epoch	34 million to 24 million years ago	Apes appeared. Camels, cats, dogs, elephants, horses, rhinoceroses, and rodents became common.
		Eocene Epoch	55 million to 34 million years ago	Birds, amphibians, small reptiles, and fish were common. Bats, camels, cats, horses, monkeys, rhinoceroses, and whales appeared.
		Paleocene Epoch	65 million to 55 million years ago	Flowering plants became common. Invertebrates, fish, amphibians, reptiles, and mammals were common.
	Cretaceous Period		145 million to 65 million years ago	Flowering plants appeared. Amphibians and invertebrates (animals without backbones) were common. Dinosaurs died out.

Scientists classify Earth's history into different divisions—called eras, periods, and epochs—and list these divisions in a chart called the geological time scale. The oldest times are at the bottom of the chart. The most recent times are at the top.

Mesozoic Era	Jurassic Period	213 million to 145 million years ago	Cone-bearing trees, squid, and huge dinosaurs were common. Birds appeared.
	Triassic Period	248 million to 213 million years ago	Cone-bearing trees, fish, and insects were common. Turtles, crocodiles, dinosaurs, and small mammals appeared.
Paleozoic Era	Permian Period	286 million to 248 million years ago	Cone-bearing trees appeared. Fish, amphibians, and reptiles were common.
	Pennsylvanian Period (also known as late Carboniferous Period)	325 million to 286 million years ago	Ferns and giant scouring rushes were common. Fish, amphibians, and giant insects were plentiful. Reptiles appeared.
	Mississippian Period (also known as early Carboniferous Period)	360 million to 325 million years ago	Most trilobites died out. Crustaceans, fish, amphibians, and coral reefs were common.
	Devonian Period	410 million to 360 million years ago	Forests grew in swamps. Many kinds of fish, such as sharks and lungfish, lived in the sea and fresh water. Amphibians and insects appeared.
	Silurian Period	440 million to 410 million years ago	Land plants bearing spores, tiny structures that can grow into new organisms, appeared. Trilobites and mollusks were common. Large coral reefs formed.
	Ordovician Period	505 million to 440 million years ago	Trilobites, corals, and mollusks were common. Tiny animals called graptolites lived in groups shaped like branches.
	Cambrian Period	544 million to 505 million years ago	Shelled animals called trilobites and mollusks became common in the sea. Jawless fish appeared.
Precambrian Time		4½ billion to 544 million years ago	Bacteria lived as long ago as 3½ billion years. Corals, jellyfish, and worms lived in the sea 1 billion years ago.

Classification of Living Things

Scientists classify animals, plants, and other living things into seven main groups, which are called kingdom, phylum (sometimes called division), class, order, family, genus, and species. These groups are listed here from largest size to smallest size. Each group is made up of the smaller groups that come after it. For example, a phylum is made up of many classes, and a class consists of many orders. The smaller the group, the more alike—and the more closely related—are the organisms in it.

The following descriptions of the groups show how a human being and a white oak tree fit into this classification system.

Kingdom

There are five kingdoms: Animalia (animals); Plantae (plants); Fungi (mushrooms, molds, and mildews); Protista (various one-celled creatures and plantlike organisms called algae); and Prokaryotae (bacteria and blue-green algae).

Phylum / Division

The animal kingdom has more than 30 different phyla (more than one phylum). All animals with backbones, including human beings, are in the phylum Chordata.

The plant kingdom has two large divisions. Simple plants make up the division Bryophyta. More complex plants, with special water-carrying tissues (such as ferns, cone-bearing trees, and flowering plants), make up the division Tracheophyta.

Class

Human beings, dogs, cats, and other animals with fur or hair are in the class Mammalia.

Flowering plants, including oak trees, make up the class Anthopsida.

Order

Human beings, apes, and monkeys make up the order Primates.

Beeches, oaks, and certain other trees make up the order Fagales.

Family

Human beings are the only living members of the family Hominidae.

Oaks and beeches belong to the family Fagaceae.

(Note that family names usually end in –ae.)

Genus

Human beings are the only living members of the genus *Homo*.

Oaks make up the genus *Quercus*.

Species

The scientific name for human beings is *Homo sapiens*. (Note that the first part of this name is the genus name. The second part is the species name.)

The white oak is *Quercus alba*.

Human Being	White Oak Tree
Kingdom: Animalia	Kingdom: Plantae
Phylum: Chordata	Phylum: Tracheophyta
Class: Mammalia	Class: Anthopsida
Order: Primate	Order: Fagales
Family: Hominidae	Family: Fagaceae
Genus: *Homo*	Genus: *Quercus*
Species: *sapiens*	Species: *alba*

Biographies of Natural Scientists

Following are brief biographies of notable natural scientists who have made important contributions in subjects covered in one or more of the volumes of *World Book's Science & Nature Guides* series. These scientists include biologists, botanists, conservationists, ecologists, entomologists, environmentalists, ethologists, geologists, horticulturists, ichthyologists, marine biologists, mineralogists, naturalists, oceanographers, ornithologists, paleontologists, taxonomists, zoologists, and other natural scientists.

Adamson, Joy

Joy Adamson (1910–1980) was a wildlife conservationist and author who won wide recognition for her observations on animal behavior in Africa. She is best known for her books *Born Free* (1960), *Living Free* (1961), and *Forever Free* (1962), in which she describes the life of the lioness Elsa. Elsa was raised in the Adamson household. She was then trained to survive in the wild by Adamson and her husband, George Adamson, a wildlife conservationist and game warden. The movie *Born Free* (1966), based on Joy Adamson's books, helped spread her message of concern for wildlife.

Joy-Friederike Victoria Gessner was born on Jan. 20, 1910, in Troppau, Silesia (now Opava, the Czech Republic). She went to Kenya at the age of 27, where she married George Adamson and lived for the rest of her life. They acquired Elsa after George had shot a lioness, Elsa's mother, in self-defense. They took Elsa and the lioness's two other orphaned cubs into their home. The couple trained Elsa to develop her natural hunting skills so that she could survive on her own. After her release into the wild, Elsa found a mate and raised three cubs.

The Adamsons were among the first conservationists to train a captive animal to establish its wild nature. They also worked to control poaching, the illegal killing of animals to obtain animal skins or the ivory of elephant tusks. In addition to living closely with lions, the Adamsons had similar experiences with cheetahs and leopards. Joy Adamson reported on these experiences in her books *The Spotted Sphinx* (1969), *Pippa's Challenge* (1972), *Joy Adamson's Africa* (1972), and *Queen of Shaba* (1980). She also wrote an autobiography, *The Searching Spirit* (1978). On Jan. 3, 1980, she died of stab wounds inflicted by a former employee. George Adamson, who worked for Kenya's wildlife department, was fatally shot by poachers on Aug. 20, 1989.

Agassiz, Louis

Louis Agassiz *(AG uh see)* (1807–1873) was a Swiss-born naturalist who studied many kinds of animals in Europe and America. He became noted for his work on both modern and fossil forms of fishes. Agassiz established a zoological laboratory on an island in Buzzards Bay off the coast of Massachusetts to provide a place to study animals in their natural surroundings. Agassiz believed that animal species do not change, and he criticized Charles Darwin's theories on evolution. As a geologist, Agassiz showed that glaciers once covered large areas of the earth.

Jean Louis Rodolphe Agassiz was born on May 28, 1807, in Motier-en-Vuly, Switzerland. He studied at the universities of Zurich, Heidelberg, and Munich. Agassiz came to the United States in 1846, and in 1848 he became a professor of zoology and geology at Harvard University. He died on Dec. 14, 1873.

Agricola, Georgius

Georgius Agricola *(JAWR jee uhs uh GRIHK uh luh)* (1494–1555) was a German physician and scientist. He became the first great mineralogist and one of the most important influences in the early history of geology. Agricola wrote seven books on geologic and mining subjects, including *Bermannus* and *On the Nature of Fossils*.

His "fossils" were mostly rocks and minerals. He described many that had not been recognized and rejected incorrect theories about others. Agricola was born on March 24, 1494, in Glauchau, in Saxony. He studied medicine in Germany and Italy.

Georgius Agricola is the Latin form of his German name, Georg Bauer. Agricola died on Nov. 21, 1555.

Andrews, Roy Chapman

Roy Chapman Andrews (1884–1960) was well known as an author and explorer, and as a leader of expeditions for the American Museum of Natural History. As a result of work from 1908 to 1914 in Alaska and Asia, he became an authority on whales. Between 1916 and 1930, Andrews led expeditions to central and eastern Asia. In the Gobi Desert, he and his co-workers found the remains of *Baluchitherium,* the largest land mammal that ever lived. They also discovered the first dinosaur eggs ever found and unearthed evidence of a prehistoric civilization.

Andrews was born on Jan. 26, 1884, in Beloit, Wisconsin, and he graduated from Beloit College. He served as Director of the American Museum of Natural History from 1935 to 1942. Andrews wrote several books, including *Whale Hunting with Gun and Camera* (1916), *The New Conquest of Central Asia (*1932), and *Beyond Adventure* (1954). He died on March 11, 1960.

Attenborough, David

David Attenborough (1926–   ) is a British naturalist, writer on natural history, and television personality. Attenborough won fame for his many television series, which explored the diversity of the world's plant and animal life.

Attenborough joined the British Broadcasting Corporation (BBC) as a trainee television producer in 1952. He began making wildlife documentaries for television in the mid-1950's. From 1954 to 1964, he made several series of TV programs for the BBC under the general title *Zoo Quest.* These programs were television expeditions to remote parts of the world. Attenborough and his crew filmed some of the rarest natural wildlife in their natural environment.

From 1965 to 1972, Attenborough was part of BBC management. He then returned to production, producing and writing such series as *Life on Earth*

(1979), *The Living Planet* (1984), and *The First Eden: Mediterranean World and Man* (1987). He also wrote and narrated an anthropology series called *The Tribal Eye* (1976). In 1977, he began narrating *Wildlife on One,* one of the longest-running natural history series in British television history. Many of his TV scripts were published in book form.

David Frederick Attenborough was born in London. Queen Elizabeth II knighted him in 1985, and he became known as Sir David Attenborough. He is the younger brother of the actor and motion-picture director and producer Richard Attenborough.

Audubon, John James

John James Audubon *(AW duh BON)* (1785–1851) was one of the first to study and paint the birds of North America. His lifelike paintings of birds in their natural surroundings brought him fame and fortune.

Audubon's diaries and letters created a mystery about his background and parentage, but records indicate that he was born Jean Rabin on April 26, 1785, at Les Cayes, Santo Domingo (now Haiti). His mother, a French chambermaid, died soon after his birth. Records show that his father, a French sea captain named Jean Audubon, remarried in France, and Jean Rabin soon joined him.

Audubon and his wife legally adopted the boy when he was 8 years old. These records disprove claims by Audubon's descendants, derived from passages in his diaries and letters, that Audubon was the Lost Dauphin of France.

In 1803, Captain Audubon sent the youth to live at Mill Grove, his estate near Philadelphia. There, young John James, as he was now called, spent much time drawing birds. He and Ferdinand Rozier opened a general store in Louisville, Kentucky, in 1807. Audubon married a Mill Grove neighbor, Lucy Bakewell, the next year. He failed in several business ventures. While Rozier conducted their business, Audubon wandered through the countryside looking for birds. His business career ended in 1819 when he was jailed for debt. He entered a plea of bankruptcy to gain his freedom.

In 1820, Audubon conceived the idea of publishing a collection of paintings of North American birds. His family followed him to

Louisiana, where he painted birds in their natural surroundings. His wife worked as a governess and teacher to support the family. Audubon drew portraits and taught music and drawing.

Unable to find an American publisher, Audubon went to England and Scotland in 1826. His pictures created a sensation, and he published *Birds of America* (1827–1838), which was a work of 87 parts containing 435 life-sized, colored engravings made from his water colors. Audubon and William MacGillivray, a Scottish naturalist, wrote a text, *Ornithological Biography* (1831–1839).

Audubon returned to the United States in 1839, and published American editions of his bird paintings. Later, Audubon worked with John Bachman on *The Viviparous Quadrupeds of North America* (1842–1854). Audubon made his last collecting trip, along the Missouri River, in 1843. He died on Jan. 27, 1851.

Bailey, Liberty Hyde

Liberty Hyde Bailey (1858–1954), an American botanist and horticulturist, was responsible more than any other person for the development of agricultural education in the United States. He served as dean of the College of Agriculture at Cornell University from 1903 to 1913 and built the college into a major institution. Bailey worked to make botanical knowledge available to farmers and gardeners, and to make botanists understand the practical problems of agriculture and horticulture. He also pioneered in plant-breeding experiments. In 1908, President Theodore Roosevelt appointed Bailey chairman of the Country Life Commission, a group that helped bring about a rural parcel post and a system of federal agricultural credit. Bailey's *Cyclopedia of American Horticulture* (1900–1902) became a standard reference book.

Bailey was born on March 15, 1858, in South Haven, Michigan. He graduated from Michigan Agricultural College (now Michigan State University). He died on Dec. 25, 1954.

Bakker, Robert T.

Robert T. Bakker (1945–   ) is a paleontologist who published the theory that dinosaurs were warm-blooded. He has popularized his work on television and in books such as *The Dinosaur Heresies* (1986).

In his expeditions around the American West, Bakker discovered 2 new species of Jurassic dinosaurs and 11 new species of early mammals. He believed that the extinction of the dinosaurs was caused by disease carried across the land bridges that appeared at the end of the Cretaceous Period. Bakker has written more than 40 professional research papers. In his novel *Raptor Red* (1995), Bakker told the imaginary tale of a year in the life of a female *Utahraptor* dinosaur.

Bakker was born on March 4, 1945, in Ridgewood, New Jersey.

Bartram, John

John Bartram *(BAHR truhm)* (1699–1777) was often called "the father of American botany." He planted the first botanical garden in America in 1728, near Philadelphia. He also collected plant specimens that allowed other naturalists to make major advances in research into North American flora.

He also helped Benjamin Franklin found the American Philosophical Society and in 1765 was named botanist to King George III.

Due to a lack of proper knowledge of grammar, Latin, and systematic botany, Bartram did not publish many of his findings. Nonetheless, he became respected for his significant contributions to botanical knowledge by the most prominent naturalists in Europe, including Carolus Linnaeus.

Bates, Henry Walter

Henry Walter Bates (1825–1892) was a British naturalist who became known for his studies on *mimicry* in insect behavior. Mimicry is the ability of a species to resemble other species or its surroundings. One type of mimicry, *Batesian mimicry,* was named after Bates. Batesian mimicry occurs when a harmless species (the *mimic)* looks like a species (the *model)* that is dangerous or annoying to its predators. The mimic species is protected from its predators only by its visual resemblance to the model species.

Bates was born in Leicester, England. He spent 11 years in South America and collected about 14,000 insect specimens. More than half of these specimens were new discoveries. He first traveled to Brazil in 1848 with his friend Alfred Russel Wallace, who was also a noted naturalist. Bates described his exploration of the Amazon Basin in his book *The Naturalist on the River Amazons* (1863). Bates's studies of insect behavior and adaptation supported the theory of evolution proposed by Wallace and also by Charles Darwin. According to this theory, animals evolve through *natural selection,* a process by which those individuals that are best suited to their environment are more likely to survive.

Beebe, William

William Beebe *(BEE bee)* (1877–1962) was a well-known American naturalist and writer. He gained fame for his vivid accounts of tropical jungles, his explorations into the depths of the sea, and his studies of birds, especially pheasants. He became curator of *ornithology* (bird study) at the New York Zoological Society in 1899. He helped found the Society's Tropical Research Department in 1916 and became the director of this department.

Beebe conducted expeditions to Borneo, British Guiana (now Guyana), and Trinidad. His many books include *Jungle Peace* (1918) and *Half Mile Down* (1934), in which he tells of his undersea adventures in an underwater observation device called a *bathysphere.* He also wrote *Beneath Tropic Seas* (1928), *Book of Bays* (1942), and *High Jungle* (1949). Beebe was born in Brooklyn, New York.

Bessey, Charles Edwin

Charles Edwin Bessey (1845-1915), an American botanist, was a great teacher whose ideas on plant evolution influenced botanical progress. From studies of fossil remains of different geological

ages, he showed that some plant structures had evolved earlier than others. He drew up a "family tree" indicating the supposed relationships between families of flowering plants. Bessey was born in Milton, Ohio. He taught botany at the University of Nebraska.

Broom, Robert

Robert Broom (1866–1951) was a Scottish anatomist and paleontologist. In 1936 in South Africa, he discovered the fossil remains of an ancient humanlike creature called *Plesianthropus,* now known as *Australopithecus africanus.* He wrote about these fossils and discussed their significance in human evolution.

Broom was born in Paisley, Scotland. He received his medical degree from Glasgow University in 1889. In 1897, he moved to South Africa. Broom practiced medicine until 1928. He was also a professor of zoology and geology at Victoria College (now Stellenbosch University) from 1903 to 1934. Broom's works include *Mammal-Like Reptiles of South Africa* (1932), *The South African Fossil Apeman* (1946), *Origin of Mammals* (1932), and *Finding the Missing Link* (1950).

Brower, David

David Brower (1912–2000), an American environmentalist, is considered by many to be the seminal leader of the American environmental movement during the last half of the 1900's.

He was nominated three times for the Nobel Peace Prize. His pioneering efforts helped to build the Sierra Club into one of the most prominent organizations in the United States and Canada that work to protect the environment.

Brower also founded or cofounded Friends of the Earth (1969), the League of Conservation Voters (1970), and Earth Island Institute (1982).

Brower led the Sierra Club's efforts to promote passage in the U.S. Congress of the Wilderness Act (1964), the first such legislation in the world, and to save or establish many national parks throughout the western United States.

Brown, Robert

Robert Brown (1773-1858) was a Scottish botanist. He was the first person to describe the general occurrence of the nucleus in living cells, and he gave it the name *nucleus.* In 1827, he described the agitation of microscopic particles that is now called *Brownian motion.* He named the world's largest flower, the *giant rafflesia* of Sumatra. This flower can grow more than 3 feet (90 centimeters) wide. Brown also began the study of plant fossils, using a microscope. Brown was born in Montrose, Scotland. He became curator at the British Museum.

Buffon, Georges-Louis Leclerc, Comte de

Georges-Louis Leclerc, Comte de Buffon *(zhawrzh lwee luh KLAIR, kawnt duh boo FOHN)* (1707–1788) was a French naturalist whose writings helped advance the study of biology and geology. His 44-volume *Histoire naturelle, generale et particuliere (Natural History, general and particular)* discussed a wide range of topics. These included the origin and development of the earth and its living things. While preparing *Histoire naturelle,* Buffon performed some of the first studies on fossils. His work led to the development of evolution as a scientific theory. Buffon was one of the first scientists to separate science completely from religious beliefs. A man of many interests, he wrote essays on such topics as mathematics, optical physics, and forestry.

Buffon was born in Montbard, near Dijon, France. After studying at the University of Angers, he became a member of the French Royal Academy of Sciences in 1734. In 1739, he was appointed director of the Royal Gardens in Paris. This appointment included supervision over the royal museums and animal menageries. Buffon wrote much of *Histoire naturelle* while serving as director.

Burbank, Luther

Luther Burbank (1849–1926) was an American plant breeder, nurseryman, and horticulturist. He introduced and developed many new fruits, vegetables, flowers, and grasses. His most famous creations include the *Burbank potato,* the *Santa Rosa plum,* and the *Shasta daisy.*

Burbank was born in Lancaster, Massachusetts. He had little opportunity for formal education but was able to attend Lancaster Academy, a college preparatory school, for a short time. He left school after his father died. He supported his mother by raising and selling vegetables.

Burbank read many works on botany by the British naturalist Charles Darwin and was influenced by Darwin's views on the evolution of plants. Burbank took a special interest in *hybrids*—that is, plants produced from breeding two kinds of plants. In his early 20's, Burbank harvested a rare seed pod of *Early Rose potato.* He planted 23 of its seeds, and they produced two promising seedlings. Burbank sold the best seedling for $150 to a nurseryman, who called it *Burbank's Seedling.* This event started Burbank on his career in plant breeding.

Burbank moved to California in 1875 and started a nursery business in Santa Rosa two years later. In 1885, he purchased a farm in nearby Sebastopol to carry out plant-breeding activities. He struck a financial bonanza with his importation of *Japanese plums* in 1885. These plums and some of Burbank's other imports were well suited to California's climate and proved especially valuable as breeding stock. In 1912, Burbank sold his past, present, and future creations to a firm that became known as the Luther Burbank Company. The company went bankrupt in less than four years and Burbank's reputation suffered. After the company declared bankruptcy, Burbank started over again and established a successful seed business.

Burbank experimented with almost 200 *genera* (groups) of plants. He became a popular national figure and did much to popularize plant breeding. A number of his creations were produced from complex *cross-pollinations* (transfers of pollens) involving many species. Burbank introduced more than 250 *cultivars* (varieties) of fruit, including 113 kinds of plums. Many of his vegetables were cultivated widely during his life. Today, the most commonly grown variety of potato in the United States is the *Russett Burbank,* a strain of the Burbank potato. Burbank's most important ornamental plant, the *Shasta daisy*, was created from crossings involving four chrysanthemum species.

Burbank cannot be considered a scientist in the academic sense. He left few records and his crossings were frequently made with mixed pollens rather than pure pollens. However, Burbank instinctively understood correct plant-breeding procedures. He made extensive crossings, grew thousands of seedlings, and continued to intercross the best seedlings to produce the most desirable hybrids. Although Burbank had no direct impact on genetics or plant breeding, his accomplishments were examples of evolution in action.

Burroughs, John

John Burroughs *(BUR ohz)* (1837–1921), an American naturalist, became widely recognized as a writer on outdoor life. Burroughs's writings made the beauties of the outdoors seem real to both children and adults. His description of birds, flowers, and a variety of natural settings in North America became increasingly poetic and philosophical over the course of his career.

Burroughs's works include the essays "Bird Enemies," "The Tragedies of the Nests," "An Idyl of the Honey-Bee," "Winter Neighbors," and "A Taste of Maine Birch." His books include *Bird and Bough* (1906), a collection of poems. Burroughs also wrote *The Light of Day* (1900), *Camping and Tramping with Roosevelt* (1907), *Time and Change* (1912), *The Summit of the Years* (1913), *The Breath of Life* (1915), and *Under the Apple-Trees* (1916).

Burroughs was born in Roxbury, New York. He spent his youth on his father's farm, working, reading, and studying. He enjoyed the works of Ralph Waldo Emerson, Walt Whitman, Matthew Arnold, and John James Audubon. Burroughs's view of nature put him in the tradition of Henry David Thoreau and Emerson.

Burroughs wrote his first book, *Notes on Walt Whitman as Poet and Person* (1867), while a clerk in the United States Department of the Treasury in Washington, D.C. He left this post in 1873 and was a bank examiner for several years. He then moved to a farm in West Park on the Hudson River, where he had a log house called Slabsides. His friends and travel companions included Theodore Roosevelt, Thomas A. Edison, and Henry Ford.

Candolle, Augustin Pyrame de

Augustin Pyrame de Candolle *(kahn DAWL)* (1778–1841), a Swiss botanist, published many books about plant classification and its theoretical aspects. His *Theorie Elementaire de la Botanique* (1813), *Regni Vegetabilis Systema Naturale* (1817-1821), and *Prodromus Systematis Naturalis Regni Vegetabilis* (begun in 1824) laid the foundations for modern studies on plant evolution and classification. De Candolle was born in Geneva.

Cousteau, Jacques-Yves

Jacques-Yves Cousteau *(zhahk eev koo stoh)* (1910–1997) was a French oceanographer, author, and motion-picture producer. He developed many techniques for undersea exploration. In 1943, Cousteau helped invent the *aqualung.* This breathing device enables a diver to move about freely underwater for long periods. Cousteau also developed the first underwater diving station and an underwater observation vehicle called the *diving saucer.*

After 1951, Cousteau explored the oceans with his research ship *Calypso.* He wrote books about sea life that have been translated into many languages. These books include *The Silent World* (1953), *The Living Sea* (1962), and *World Without Sun* (1964). He produced many films about sea life, three of which won Academy Awards.

In 1960, Cousteau and Prince Rainier III of Monaco opposed France's plan to dump radioactive wastes into the Mediterranean Sea. France abandoned the plan that year. During the 1960's and 1970's, Cousteau's television series,

"The Undersea World of Jacques Cousteau," dramatized underwater exploration and the need for conservation of ocean life. In 1974, Cousteau started the Cousteau Society to protect ocean life.

Cousteau was born on June 11, 1910, in St.-Andre-de-Cubzac, which is near Bordeaux. He died on June 25, 1997.

Cuvier, Baron

Baron Cuvier *(KOO vee AY* or *koov YAY)* (1769–1832) was a French naturalist who studied *comparative anatomy,* a branch of zoology that compares the differences and similarities in the body structure of different animals. Cuvier included investigations of the remains of prehistoric animals in his comparisons. He wrote *The Animal Kingdom* (1817), which became an authoritative reference on the classification of animals.

Cuvier began his work by dissecting marine *invertebrates* (animals without backbones). He later studied many large land mammals, including the rhinoceros and the elephant. Cuvier proposed the theory of *geological catastrophe* to explain why many fossil animals no longer exist. This theory held that great volcanic upheavals and similar catastrophes destroyed many forms of life. Cuvier believed that the distinctive anatomical characters of various animal groups was proof that they had not evolved from the same ancestor. Cuvier also believed that species did not change over time.

Georges Leopold Chretien Frederic Dagobert Cuvier was born in Montbeliard, France. He taught at the College of France. He helped found some of the French provincial universities.

Dana, James Dwight

James Dwight Dana (1813–1895) was an American geologist, mineralogist, and zoologist. He was mineralogist and geologist of a government exploring expedition in the Pacific Ocean under Lieutenant Charles Wilkes from 1838 to 1842. He also collected and studied corals and *crustaceans* (hard-shelled water creatures). He was a professor at Yale from 1856 to 1890.

Later, he became editor in chief of the *American Journal of Science.* His most important books were *System of Mineralogy, Manual of Geology,* and *On Corals and Coral Islands.* He was born in Utica, New York, and graduated from Yale University.

Darwin, Charles Robert

Charles Robert Darwin (1809–1882) was a British naturalist who became famous for his theories on evolution. Like several other scientists before him, Darwin believed that, through millions of years, all species of plants and animals had *evolved* (developed gradually) from a few common ancestors.

Darwin's theories included several related ideas. They were (1) that evolution had occurred; (2) that most evolutionary change was gradual, requiring thousands or millions of years; (3) that the primary mechanism for evolution was a process called *natural selection,* and (4) that the millions of species present on Earth today arose from a single original life form through a branching process called *speciation,* by which one species can give rise to two or more species. Darwin set forth his theories in his book *On the Origin of Species by Means of Natural Selection, or the Preservation of Favoured Races in the Struggle for Life* (1859).

Darwin's theories shocked most people of his day, who believed that each species had been created by a separate divine act. His book, which is usually called simply *The Origin of Species,* presented facts that refuted this belief. It caused a revolution in biological science and greatly affected religious thought.

Darwin was born in Shrewsbury, England, on Feb. 12, 1809. He was the grandson of the noted physician and naturalist Erasmus Darwin, who had proposed a theory of evolution in the 1790's. As a boy, Charles often heard his grandfather's theories discussed.

Darwin studied medicine at the University of Edinburgh and theology at Cambridge University. He received a bachelor's degree from Cambridge in 1831. From 1831 to 1836, Darwin served as a naturalist with a British scientific expedition aboard the H.M.S. *Beagle.* The expedition visited places throughout the world, and he studied plants and animals everywhere it went.

In South America, Darwin found fossils of extinct animals that closely resembled modern species. On the Galapagos Islands in the Pacific Ocean, he noticed many variations among plants and animals of the same general type as those in South America. He collected the fossils and other specimens for future study.

Darwin returned to England in 1836 and settled in London. He spent the rest of his life studying specimens, doing experiments, corresponding with other scientists, and writing about his findings. Darwin's early books included *The Structure and Distribution of Coral Reefs* (1842) and a journal of his research aboard the *Beagle*.

In 1839, Darwin married his cousin Emma Wedgwood. The family moved to Downe, near Croydon, in 1842, and Darwin lived there until his death.

The study of the specimens from the voyage of the *Beagle* convinced Darwin that modern species had evolved from a few earlier ones. He documented the evidence and first presented his theories on evolution to a meeting of scientists in 1858.

In most cases, according to Darwin, no two members of any species are exactly alike. Each organism has an individual combination of traits, and many of these traits are inherited. Darwin claimed that gardeners and farmers commonly developed special kinds of plants and animals by selecting and breeding organisms that had desired traits. He believed a similar selective process took place in nature. Darwin called this process *natural selection,* and others have called it the *survival of the fittest*.

Darwin showed that living things commonly produce many more offspring than are necessary to replace themselves. The earth cannot possibly support all these organisms, and so they must compete for such necessities as food and shelter. Their lives also are threatened by animals that prey on them, by unfavorable weather, and by other environmental conditions.

Darwin suggested that some members of a species have traits that aid them in this struggle for life. Other members have less favorable traits and therefore are less likely to survive or reproduce. On the average, the members with favorable traits live longer and produce more offspring than do the others. They also pass on the favorable traits to their young. The unfavorable traits are eventually eliminated. When this process occurs in two isolated populations of one species, members of one species may become so genetically different that they will be regarded as separate species.

Darwin wrote several books that further discussed his theories of evolution. These included *The Descent of Man and Selection in Relation to Sex* (1871) and *The Expression of the Emotions in Man and Animals* (1872).

Darwin's theories of evolution through natural selection set off a bitter controversy among biologists, religious leaders, and the general public. Many people thought Darwin had implied that human beings were descended from monkeys, and they angrily criticized his revolutionary ideas. But such noted British scientists as Thomas Henry Huxley and Alfred Russel Wallace supported Darwin's work, and virtually all scientists eventually accepted his theories. These theories, and the facts that supported them, gave biologists new insight into the origin of living things and the relationship among various species.

Darwin's theories stimulated studies in biology, particularly in paleontology and comparative anatomy. During the first half of the 1900's, discoveries in genetics and developmental biology were used as evidence for theories of evolution that regarded natural selection as unimportant. But after World War II ended in 1945, Darwin's theories again became the dominant influence in evolutionary biology in a form often called *Neo-Darwinism*. Neo-Darwinism gave a fuller explanation for the genetic origin of variation within species and for how species are formed. Few biologists reject the basic propositions of Neo-Darwinism, and Darwin's theories are still the basis for many biological studies.

Darwin's work has had a tremendous impact on religious thought. Many people strongly oppose the idea of evolution—and the teaching of it—because it conflicts with their religious beliefs. For example, they claim that the theory of evolution disagrees with the Biblical account of the Creation. Some people argue against the theory of natural selection because they believe it diminishes the role of divine guidance in the universe.

Darwin avoided discussing the theological and sociological aspects of his work, but other writers used his ideas in their own theories about society. The German philosopher Karl Marx compared the struggle for survival among organisms to the struggle for power among social classes. Certain other writers referred to natural selection to justify the concept of the development of superior races of human beings. Scholars called social Darwinists used Darwin's ideas to promote the belief that people in a society—and societies themselves—must compete for survival.

Darwin died on April 19, 1882. He was buried in Westminster Abbey in London.

Dawkins, Richard

Richard Dawkins (1941–) is one of the United Kingdom's best-known popular scientists. His books about evolutionary biology, which include *The Selfish Gene* (1976), *The Blind Watchmaker* (1986), *River Out of Eden* (1995), *Climbing Mount Improbable* (1996), and *Unweaving the Rainbow* (1998), became best sellers. He was appointed professor of public understanding of science at Oxford University in 1996.

Clinton Richard Dawkins was born on March 26, 1941, in Nairobi, Kenya. He studied zoology at Oxford University. He taught at the University of California, in the United States, then returned to Oxford University to teach. For a while, he was presenter of the British Broadcasting Corporation television program *Horizon.*

Dawson, George Mercer

George Mercer Dawson (1849–1901) was a Canadian geologist and the son of the geologist Sir John William Dawson. George Dawson joined the Geological Survey of Canada in 1875 and became its director in 1895. The Survey published much of his work, including the first detailed investigations of the geology and natural resources of British Columbia and the Yukon (now the Yukon Territory). Dawson also published geographical descriptions of Canada and was coauthor of a study of Indian languages. During the 1870's, he called attention to the rich beds of dinosaur fossils located in Alberta.

Dawson was born in Pictou, Nova Scotia. He attended McGill University in Montreal and the Royal School of Mines in London. Dawson, the capital of the Yukon Territory from 1898 to 1953, is named for him.

Dawson, John William

John William Dawson (1820–1899) was a Canadian geologist and educator. His major work was *Acadian Geology* (first published in 1855), a study of rock formations in Nova Scotia. The book vigorously opposed the theory of naturalist Louis Agassiz that a huge sheet of ice once covered large regions of the Northern Hemisphere. Dawson incorrectly believed that glaciers had covered only small areas of the earth.

Dawson also wrote about coal deposits and the fossils they contain. He discovered important early amphibians and reptiles. In addition, Dawson published on natural history, agriculture, evolution, fossils, and the relationship between science and religion.

Dawson was born in Pictou, Nova Scotia. He served as principal of McGill University in Montreal from 1855 to 1893. In 1882, Dawson became the first president of the Royal Society of Canada.

De Vries, Hugo

Hugo de Vries *(duh VREES)* (1848–1935), a Dutch botanist and student of organic evolution, was known primarily as the author of the *mutation theory.* This theory states that new species of plants and animals arise by *mutations* (sudden transformations), which might appear at any time and are then continued from generation to generation. De Vries's work stimulated research on heredity and evolution. However, mutations as conspicuous as those he described in the evening primrose were later proved to be the exception, not the rule. Born in Haarlem, the Netherlands, de Vries became famous with the publication of *The Mutation Theory* (1901–1903). He also wrote *Intracellular Pangenesis* (1889), and *Plant Breeding* (1907).

Ditmars, Raymond Lee

Raymond Lee Ditmars (1876–1942) was a noted American authority on reptiles. His popular books included *The Reptile Book* (1907) and *Reptiles of the World* (1910). He became curator of reptiles at the New York Zoological Park in 1899 and remained at the park until his death. He pioneered in developing snake-bite serums, which have saved many lives. Ditmars was born in Newark, New Jersey.

Durrell, Gerald

Gerald Durrell *(DOOR uhl)* (1925–1995) was a British naturalist and author. He was best known for his work in wildlife preservation and his books on animals. Durrell described his experiences with animals in light-hearted stories. Many are popular with young readers.

Durrell was born on Jan. 7, 1925, in Jamshedpur, India, of British parents. He was educated in Europe by private tutors. In 1947, Durrell began a career of leading zoological expeditions. He traveled to Cameroon, Madagascar, Mexico, Australia, and other places to collect animals for zoos in Europe and North America. Durrell began writing to help finance his expeditions. His first book was *The Overloaded Ark* (1953).

In the mid-1950's, Durrell decided to create his own zoo. He opened his zoo in Jersey, England, in 1959 and dedicated it to breeding endangered species. This zoo is known as the Jersey Zoological Park and is now operated by the Jersey Wildlife Preservation Trust.

Durrell eventually wrote more than 30 books. Besides *The Overloaded Ark,* they include *A Zoo in My Luggage* (1960) and *The Stationary Ark* (1976).

He also wrote *The Amateur Naturalist* (1983) with his wife, Lee. He died on Jan. 30, 1995.

Elton, Charles Sutherland

Charles Sutherland Elton (1900–1991) was an English biologist. He was known as a pioneer in establishing the science of *ecology,* which deals with the relation of living things to their environment and to one another.

Elton recognized that animal species and populations fit together in their environment to form communities. He recognized the concept of *ecological niche*—the idea that each species has a unique function and place within the environment. Elton also pointed out that a large number of plants are needed to supply food for a smaller number of plant-eating animals. Such animals, in turn, provide food for an even smaller number of meat-eating creatures. Elton called this natural system of food relationships a *pyramid of numbers.*

Elton was born on March 29, 1900, in Manchester and graduated from Oxford University in 1922. He taught animal ecology at Oxford from 1932 until he retired in 1967. Elton wrote *Animal Ecology* (1927), *The Ecology of Invasions by Animals and Plants* (1958), and *The Pattern of Animal Communities* (1966). He died on May 1, 1991.

Fabre, Jean Henri Casimir

Jean Henri Casimir Fabre *(zhahn ahn REE ka zee MEER FAH buhr)* (1823–1915), a French naturalist, spent his life observing insects and spiders. He wrote simply of what he saw in the gardens and fields near his home. He received the ribbon of the Legion of Honor but was fired from his teaching position because he allowed girls to attend his science classes. Fabre was almost unknown outside of France until he was nearly 80. Then the great scientific societies recognized his work. He wrote a 10-volume *Souvenirs Entomologiques.* In addition to his scholarly works on insects, Fabre wrote approximately 40 works on popular science topics, mostly for young readers. Fabre was born on Dec. 22, 1823, in St. Leon. He died on Oct. 11, 1915.

Fairchild, David Grandison

David Grandison Fairchild (1869–1954), an American botanist and explorer, traveled the world and brought more than 20,000 species of plants back to the United States. He helped found the Section of Foreign Seed and Plant Introduction in the U.S. Department of Agriculture and directed that section from 1906 to 1928. In 1938, he established the Fairchild Tropical Garden near Miami, Florida. It became one of the world's most extensive botanical gardens. Fairchild wrote such books as *Exploring for Plants* (1930), *The World Was My Garden* (1938), *Garden Islands of the Great East* (1945), and *The World Grows Round My Door* (1947).

Fairchild was born on April 7, 1869, in Lansing, Michigan. He studied at Kansas State and Iowa State colleges and at Rutgers University. He began collecting plants during a voyage around the world from 1897 to 1905. He died on Aug. 6, 1954.

Fleay, David

David Fleay (1907–1993), an Australian zoologist, was the first person to breed a platypus (an unusual, egg-laying mammal) in captivity in 1944. He was considered one of the world's greatest authorities on the platypus. Fleay was also the first person to milk a taipan (Australia's largest venomous snake) to produce an *antivenin* (an antitoxin used to counteract snake venom) in 1950.

David Howells Fleay was born at Ballarat, in Victoria, Australia. He became director of the Sir Colin MacKenzie sanctuary (now the Healesville Sanctuary) in Healesville, Victoria. At the sanctuary, Fleay and his staff studied rare and well-known Australian species, including the common wombat, wedge-tailed eagles, possum gliders, and tree kangaroos. In 1944, they celebrated the birth of the first platypus born in captivity.

In 1952, Fleay established a wildlife sanctuary in Burleigh Heads, Queensland. Fleay was the director of this sanctuary until the early 1980's, when he turned the facility over to the Queensland Parks and Wildlife Service. Today, the sanctuary (now named the David Fleay Wildlife Park) is a popular destination for tourists and school groups, as well as a research center. Many of the animals at the Wildlife Park are endangered or threatened.

For many years, Fleay wrote a nature column for a Brisbane newspaper, the *Courier-Mail.* He also wrote a number of books, including *Living with Animals* (1960). He cofounded the Wildlife Preservation Society of Queensland. The giant frog, *Mixophyes fleayi,* was named after him.

Fossey, Dian

Dian Fossey (1932–1985) was an American zoologist who studied the mountain gorillas of the Virunga Mountains in east-central Africa. She founded the Karisoke Research Center in Rwanda and lived there in near-isolation for almost 18 years. Fossey's research on wild mountain gorillas led to efforts to protect this rare and endangered species. She was mysteriously murdered at her camp in Rwanda in December 1985.

Fossey was born on Jan. 16, 1932, in San Francisco. She received a bachelor's degree in occupational therapy from San Jose State College (now San Jose State University) in 1954. In 1963, inspired by a book about mountain gorillas by American zoologist George Schaller, Fossey borrowed money and traveled to Africa to see the animals. There, Fossey visited the camp of British anthropologist Louis Leakey. In 1966, Leakey picked Fossey to begin a long-term field study of the animals. Fossey received a doctorate for her gorilla research from Cambridge University in Cambridge, England, in 1974.

To gain acceptance by the mountain gorillas, Fossey imitated their habits and sounds. She studied them daily and came to know each animal individually. After several of her favorite mountain gorillas were killed, Fossey focused on protecting the animals from poachers and from the destruction of their mountain habitat. Some United States officials believe Fossey may have been murdered by poachers angered by her strong attempts to protect the animals. Fossey described her research in the book *Gorillas in the Mist* (1983). A motion picture about her with the same title was released in 1988.

Galdikas, Biruté

Biruté Galdikas *(bih ROO tay GAHL duh kuhs)* (1946–   ), a Lithuanian-born Canadian anthropologist, is one of the world's leading experts on orangutans. Since 1971, she has studied wild orangutans on the Southeast Asian island of Borneo.

Galdikas's early field work focused on how orangutans reproduce and interact with one another. These studies helped determine that orangutans differ from their ape relatives— chimpanzees, bonobos, and gorillas—in that they lead basically solitary lives. Males live alone except for brief periods when they mate with females. Adult females often live only with their offspring. Later work done by Galdikas and her colleagues revealed much about the orangutans' extensive diet, which consists of more than 400 types of foods. Galdikas also studied the apes' elaborate communication system and their ability to learn and solve problems.

Biruté Marija Filomena Galdikas was born on May 10, 1946, in Wiesbaden, Germany, to Lithuanian parents. She grew up in Toronto. Galdikas received her Ph.D. degree in anthropology from the University of California at Los Angeles (UCLA) in 1978.

In addition to her scientific contributions, Galdikas has led the effort to conserve orangutans and their dwindling rain forest habitat. As part of this effort, she instituted a program to reintroduce captive orangutans back into the wild. She also serves as president of the Orangutan Foundation International, a conservation organization based in Los Angeles. Galdikas spends part of each year teaching in Canada, at Simon Fraser University in Burnaby, British Columbia, where she is professor of archaeology. Her writings include the book *Reflections of Eden: My Years with the Orangutans of Borneo* (1995) and numerous articles. She also coauthored the book *Orangutan Odyssey* (1999).

Goodall, Jane

Jane Goodal (1934–   ) is an English zoologist who studies the behavior of animals. She became known for her work with chimpanzees and her

efforts to ensure their survival in the wild. Goodall began her research in 1960 at what is now Gombe Stream National Park in northwestern Tanzania. She won the trust of many chimpanzees through daily contact with them. She observed them at close range and wrote detailed reports.

Before Goodall's research, scientists believed that chimpanzees ate chiefly fruits and vegetables and, occasionally, insects and small rodents. But Goodall found that chimpanzees also hunt and eat larger animals, including young monkeys and pigs. She also discovered that they make and use tools more than any other animal except human beings. Goodall observed them stripping tree twigs and using the twigs as tools for catching termites. She also observed the first known instance where one group of chimpanzees systematically killed off another group for no obvious survival reason. Goodall's research surprised most naturalists because it suggests that such behaviors as hunting, tool use, and "warfare" are not unique to human beings.

Goodall wrote many books, including *My Friends, the Wild Chimpanzees* (1967), *In the Shadow of Man* (1971), *The Chimpanzees of Gombe* (1986), *The Chimpanzee Family Book* (1989), *Through a Window: My Thirty Years with the Chimpanzees of the Gombe* (1990), *Visions of Caliban: On Chimpanzees and People* (with Dale Peterson, 1993), *Reason for Hope: A Spiritual Journey* (1999), *Beyond Innocence: An Autobiography in Letters: The Later Years* (Dale Peterson, editor, 2001). She has also produced numerous films on the Gombe chimpanzees.

In 1986, she and several colleagues founded the Committee for the Conservation and Care of Chimpanzees. As the organization's principal spokesperson, she spent two years lobbying the United States government to give added protection to chimpanzees by reclassifying them as an "endangered" rather than a "threatened" species. Endangered species face the most serious threat of extinction, requiring direct human protection for survival. Threatened species face serious but not immediate danger of extinction.

Valerie Jane Goodall was born on April 3, 1934, in London. She earned a Ph.D. degree from

Cambridge University. In 2003, Goodall was made a Dame Commander of the Order of the British Empire and became known as Dame Jane Goodall.

Gould, John

John Gould (1804–1881), a British ornithologist, produced illustrated books on birds from every part of the world. Gould was born in Dorset, England. He began work as a gardener and later became a taxidermist with the Zoological Society of London. Working with bird skins received from the Himalaya, he wrote *A Century of Birds from the Himalaya Mountains* (1831-1832). Gould visited Australia from 1838 to 1840. With the paintings of birds made by his wife, Elizabeth, Gould completed *The Birds of Australia,* published in seven volumes, in 1848. It became his most famous work.

Gould, Stephen Jay

Stephen Jay Gould *(goold)* (1941–2002) was an American scientist and educator. He wrote widely on *paleontology*, the scientific study of animals, plants, and other organisms that lived in prehistoric times. Gould was best known for his writings on the *evolution* (development) of life on Earth. He questioned the traditional idea that evolution is a gradual and continuous process. He suggested that evolution occurs in rapid, irregular spurts, a process called "punctuated equilibrium."

Gould did much to make scientific subjects understandable to nonscientists. He did this largely through essays, including some on such topics as baseball and Mickey Mouse. Many of these essays appeared in his books *Ever Since Darwin* (1977), *The Panda's Thumb* (1980), *Hen's Teeth and Horse's Toes* (1983), *The Flamingo's Smile* (1985), *Bully for Brontosaurus* (1991), *Dinosaur in a Haystack* (1995), and *The Lying Stones of Marrakech* (2000). Other books by Gould include *The Mismeasure of Man* (1981), *Wonderful Life* (1990), *Full House* (1996), and *Rocks of Ages* (1999).

Gould was born in New York City on Sept. 10, 1941. He graduated from Antioch College and earned a Ph.D. degree in paleontology from

Columbia University. Gould taught at Harvard University since 1967. He died on May 20, 2002.

Gray, Asa

Asa Gray (1810–1888) was the leading authority of his time on plant life in the United States. Gray specialized in the classification and description of plants and gained fame for interpreting the plant life of past geological ages. *Gray's Manual of Botany,* which was first published in 1848, helped to increase knowledge of plants growing in the northeastern United States and to popularize botany.

He believed that each plant species originated in one place, and that physical means, such as wind, spread a plant species from its point of origin. In his own studies, Gray found evidence that supported the British naturalist Charles Darwin's principles of evolution, and he vigorously defended Darwin's ideas.

Gray was born in Sauquoit, New York, on Nov. 18, 1810. He became interested in botany while studying medicine, and spent his spare time roaming the countryside in search of plants. He received his medical degree from Fairfield Medical College in Herkimer County, New York, in 1831 but never practiced. He taught science in Utica, New York, and in 1836, he became curator at the New York Lyceum of Natural History. Two years later, he was appointed professor of natural history at the University of Michigan. In 1842, he became professor of natural history at Harvard University and stayed there until his death on Jan. 30, 1888. His library and herbarium formed the nucleus of the Harvard University Herbaria, one of the largest and most noted in the world.

Haeckel, Ernst Heinrich

Ernst Heinrich Haeckel *(HYN rihk HEHK uhl)* (1834–1919), a German zoologist, became known for his theory of *recapitulation*. This theory, no longer held by most zoologists, states that each animal during its growth as an embryo repeats the changes its ancestors underwent. For example, if a land animal had ancestors that lived in water and used gills, then each embryo of that animal continues to develop gills as did its ancestors, even though the gills may be lost during later embryonic development.

Haeckel also coined the word "ecology," which he defined as "the comprehensive science of relationships of the organism to the environment."

Haeckel's works in zoology included descriptions of about 4,000 new species of lower marine animals, especially radiolarians. His ability to draw and paint helped to correctly classify the species. He used his findings to support Charles Darwin's theory of evolution. Haeckel was the first to draw a "family tree" of animal life, showing the supposed relationships of animal groups.

His widely read book, *The Riddle of the Universe* (1899), explained many of his theories. His early work included a study of marine organisms, chiefly radiolarians, coelenterates, and echinoderms. Other literary works include *General Morphology* (1866), *Natural History of Creation* (1868), and *Anthropogenie* (1874).

Haeckel was born in Potsdam, Germany, on Feb. 16, 1834. He liked botany but studied medicine at his father's insistence. He was educated at Wurzburg, Vienna, and Berlin universities. He served as a professor of zoology at the University of Jena from 1862 to 1909. He died in Jena on Aug. 9, 1919.

Hall, James, Jr.

James Hall, Jr. (1811–1898), an American *paleontologist* (specialist in fossils), was one of the most influential scientists of his time. His greatest work was a 13-volume *Palaeontology of New York,* which was written over a period of 50 years. Hall also published many other reports, maps, and technical papers.

Hall directed, and often paid, a large staff of assistants whom he trained as paleontologists. He built up three private collections of fossils. The third of his collections became the New York State Museum.

Hall was born at Hingham, Massachusetts. He graduated from the Rensselaer School (now Rensselaer Polytechnic Institute) in New York.

Hendrickson, Sue

Sue Hendrickson (1949–) is an American-born fossil-hunter, commercial diver, and prospector. She discovered the largest and most complete *Tyrannosaurus rex* ever found.

Hendrickson was born in Chicago and grew up in Munster, Indiana. In 1974, Hendrickson traveled to the Dominican Republic with a team of divers. On a return trip, she visited an amber mine and saw a fossil insect preserved in amber. She became a dedicated fossil-hunter and discovered many amber fossils, including specimens of three 23-million-year-old butterflies.

Hendrickson later joined paleontologist Kirby Siber and his team on six winter digs for whale fossils in Peru. There, in 1985, she met Peter Larson, president of The Black Hills Institute for Geological Research, a fossil-finding company. Hendrickson volunteered with his group.

In summer 1990, Hendrickson discovered three vertebrae of a *Tyrannosaurus rex* sticking out of a cliff 8 miles (13 kilometers) from the institute's base camp in Faith, South Dakota. Hendrickson and the institute team spent more than two weeks removing a 29-foot (8.8-meter) layer of rock above the skeleton, which turned out to be the largest, most complete, and best preserved *T. rex* ever found. The skeleton was named Sue in her honor.

Holmes, Arthur

Arthur Holmes (1890–1965) was a British geologist who used radioactivity to determine the age of rocks, which led to new estimations of the earth's age.

While doing postgraduate studies on rocks, Holmes compared the amounts of the radioactive elements uranium and thorium to figure out geological time. He figured the minimum age of the earth to be 1,600 million years. In 1929, Holmes proposed a modification of Alfred

Wegener's theory on continental drift. He believed the cause of the earth's movements was subcrustal convection currents. He theorized that the continental rocks were lighter and resisted being submerged and that the heavier oceanic rocks were pushed back down to the mantle. New evidence eventually helped support his theory.

His best-known and most important work, *Principles of Physical Geology* was well received because it helped clarify the confusing field of geology.

Hooker, William Jackson

William Jackson Hooker (1785–1865) was an English botanist, prolific author, and gifted botanical illustrator. He became the first director of the Royal Botanic Gardens at Kew in 1841, upon the park's presentation to the nation.

While still in his 20's, he began an herbarium at Halesworth. He expanded his herbarium over the years into the largest and most valuable privately held herbarium in the country. The herbarium at his house *West Park* attracted a host of international scientists and ultimately occupied 13 rooms, contained a million specimens of dried plants, and had a library of more than 4,000 books.

Aside from writing, illustrating, and editing *Curtis's Botanical Magazine*, Hooker contributed to other journals. He also wrote numerous books on botany, including *British Jungermanniae*, which made his reputation and is considered his most beautiful work. In 1820, he became regius professor of botany at Glasgow University, and along with his teaching duties there, he expanded the city's botanic garden from 8,000 plant species to 20,000.

In 1820, he also began a long battle to see the Royal Botanic Gardens at Kew established as a national botanic garden. He succeeded in 1840 and became the gardens' first director the next year. Throughout the rest of his life, Hooker built Kew into one of the world's leading botanic gardens. The gardens were opened to the public in 1841.

In 1847, Hooker also established the popular Museum of Economic Botany. The first museum of its kind, it displayed specimens of vegetable products and materials for craftsmen, tradesmen, and manufacturers. The museum contained so many exhibits that by 1863 it had expanded to fill three separate buildings.

Horner, Jack

Jack Horner (1946–) is an American paleontologist who has made many discoveries of dinosaur fossils. In the summer of 2000, he led an expedition that uncovered five *Tyrannosaurus rex* skeletons. This remarkable number in such a short time suggested that the *T. rex* was more common than scientists had believed. Prior to that, a total of only 20 had been unearthed worldwide.

John "Jack" Horner was raised in Shelby, Montana. In 1982, he became curator of paleontology at the Museum of the Rockies in Bozeman, Montana. He equipped his museum laboratory with advanced technology to allow detailed study of fossils. Horner calls himself a *paleobiologist,* as he seeks to understand the biology of prehistoric creatures. In his microscopic examination of bones, for instance, blood vessel patterns supported the view of some paleontologists that dinosaurs were warm-blooded, although strictly speaking they were neither warm- nor cold-blooded, but had a type of metabolism not found in animals today.

In the early 1990's, Horner unearthed one of the most complete *T. rex* skeletons ever found, with its unusually small arm bones intact. He discovered the first dinosaur eggs in North America and the first dinosaur embryos. In 1982, he discovered a bone bed containing more than 10,000 duckbill dinosaur fossils.

Horner served as a technical adviser for the films *Jurassic Park* (1993) and its sequel *The Lost World* (1997) and often appears in television specials. He has written many papers and popular articles. He cowrote the book *Digging Up Tyrannosaurus Rex* (1992) and wrote *Dinosaurs: Under the Big Sky* (2001) about Montana's dinosaurs and geologic history.

Huxley, Julian Sorell

Julian Sorell Huxley (1887–1975) was a noted British biologist. He did research in *ornithology* (the study of birds) and on the experimental analysis of development. He made a study of the relative rates of growth of bodily organs and developed a mathematical method to analyze body proportions. His book *Evolution, the Modern Synthesis* (1942) unites theories of evolution with modern theories of genetic inheritance.

In 1946, Huxley helped establish the United Nations Educational, Scientific and Cultural Organization (UNESCO). He was elected the agency's first director-general in 1946. In 1958, he was knighted for his contributions to science.

Huxley's writings include *Essays of a Biologist* (1923), *The Science of Life* (with H. G. Wells and G. P. Wells, 1929–1930), *Problems of Relative Growth* (1932), *Elements of Experimental Embryology* (with G. R. de Beer, 1934), *Man Stands Alone* (1941), *Man in the Modern World* (1947), and *Essays of a Humanist* (with H. B. Kettlewell, 1964). He also wrote several poems.

Huxley was born on June 22, 1887, in London. He taught at Rice Institute in Texas from 1912 to 1916. He later became a professor at King's College, London. He died on Feb. 14, 1975. Huxley was a grandson of British scientist Thomas Henry Huxley.

Jordan, David Starr

David Starr Jordan (1851–1931) was an American educator, naturalist, and *ichthyologist* (scientist who studies fish) who named 1,085 genera and more than 2,500 species of fish as well as their broader classifications. After teaching in Illinois, Wisconsin, and Indiana, he became president of Indiana University in 1885. He became Stanford University's first president in 1891 and built the school into an important institution. After he retired in 1916, Jordan devoted much time and energy to the cause of international peace and was chief director of the World Peace Foundation. He was born in Gainesville, New York, and graduated from Cornell University with a master's degree in 1872.

Lamarck, Chevalier de

Chevalier de Lamarck (SHEV *uh LIHR duh luh MAHRK*) (1744–1829) was a French biologist and botanist. He was one of the first scientists to propose a theory of biological evolution. Lamarck was also a founder of *invertebrate paleontology* (the study of prehistoric animals without backbones).

Lamarck began his work as a botanist in the late 1760's. In 1779 he published a system of plant classification. In the 1790's, he transferred his interest from botany to zoology and soon developed a system for classifying invertebrate animals.

From his work in botany and zoology, Lamarck concluded that plants and animals change their forms to adapt to their environment, and that these changes are then passed along to their offspring. These ideas influenced Charles Darwin in his development of the theory of evolution. Lamarck's theory was disproved by discoveries in genetics in the early 1900's, when it was shown that acquired characteristics of an organism cannot be genetically transmitted to its offspring.

In addition to these studies, Lamarck was the first scientist to try to forecast the weather. He published an annual meteorological report from 1799 to 1810. It is said that he was responsible for the names of the various cloud types: *cirrus, stratus, cumulus,* and *nimbus.*

Lamarck was born Jean Baptiste Pierre Antoine de Monet in Bazentin, Picardy. He inherited the title Chevalier de Lamarck from his father. Lamarck studied briefly for the priesthood, then served as an army officer during the Seven Years' War (1756–1763). Later, he turned for a short time to medicine. In 1768, he began studying under the noted botanist Bernard de Jussieu. He became conservator of the royal herbarium in Paris in 1788, and he was appointed professor of zoology at the Museum of Natural History there in 1793. In his later years, Lamarck was completely blind, but he continued his work with the assistance of others.

Leakey, Richard Erskine Frere

Richard Erskine Frere Leakey (1944–   ) is a Kenyan paleoanthropologist who has continued the work of his famous parents, anthropologists Louis Seymour Bazett Leakey and Mary Douglas Leakey, uncovering the mysteries of human origins. In his lifetime, he has unearthed some of the most spectacular early hominid fossils ever found, and he has worked on conservationist and political issues related to his native Kenya.

He served as director of the National Museums of Kenya from 1968 until 1989 and director of the Kenya Wildlife Service from 1989 until 1994, and again in 1998. His efforts almost single-handedly brought about a ban on the exportation of ivory, thus saving Kenya's remaining elephant population.

Leakey is most associated with numerous paleoanthropological discoveries, including ER 1470 (registration number), a skull of *Homo habilis* found in 1972, and, in 1984, the Turkana Boy, WT 15000, a nearly complete skeleton of *Homo erectus,* dated at about 1.5 million years old. These outstanding finds were all uncovered in his primary excavation site, around Kenya's Lake Turkana.

Leopold, Aldo

Aldo Leopold (1887–1948) was an American naturalist, wildlife biologist, and conservationist. He pioneered the application of ecological principles to wildlife management. An enthusiastic outdoorsman, he believed that people should enjoy wilderness areas for recreation. But he declared that the natural characteristics of such areas should be preserved as much as possible.

Leopold wrote both books and articles that emphasized conservation. His textbook *Game Management* (1933) is considered a classic. *A Sand County Almanac* (1949) and *Round River* (1953) include many of Leopold's philosophic essays on conservation. These essays stress the need for wilderness areas.

Leopold was born on Jan. 11, 1887, in Burlington, Iowa. He graduated from Yale University in 1908 and earned a Master of Forestry degree there the next year. He worked for the U.S. Forest Service from 1909 to 1927. He was a member of the faculty of the University of Wisconsin from 1933 until his death on April 21,

1948. A biography, *Aldo Leopold: His Life and Work,* was published in 1987.

Linnaeus, Carolus

Carolus Linnaeus *(KAR uh luhs lih NEE uhs)* (1707–1778), a Swedish naturalist and botanist, established the modern scientific method of naming plants and animals. In this system, each living thing has a name with two parts. The first part of the name is for the *genus* (group). The second part is for the *species* (kind). Linnaeus's book *Species Plantarum* (1753) forms the basis for plant classification. The 10th edition of his *Systema Naturae* (1758) covers animal classification.

Linnaeus was born on May 23, 1707, in Rashult, near Kristianstad, Sweden. His father, the parish curate, wanted him to study for the ministry. But the boy was so interested in plants that friends urged his parents to send him to medical school. While in medical school, Linnaeus supervised a small botanical garden and began an insect collection. He wrote careful descriptions of all the kinds of plants he knew, and these notes formed the basis for his books. He became famous as Carolus Linnaeus because he wrote his books in Latin.

With $50 given to him by the Royal Society of Science, he spent five months in 1732 collecting plants in Lapland. During this trip, he walked nearly 1,000 miles (1,600 kilometers). Linnaeus then went to the Netherlands, where he received his medical degree. When he returned to Stockholm to practice medicine, the Swedish government gave him a position. Linnaeus became a professor of botany at Uppsala University in 1742. In 1758, he was granted Swedish nobility and changed his name to Carl von Linne. He died at Uppsala on Jan. 10, 1778.

Lorenz, Konrad Zacharias

Konrad Zacharias Lorenz *(KOHN raht TSAH kah REE ahs LOH rehnts)* (1903–1989), an Austrian naturalist, was one of the founders of *ethology,* the study of animal behavior. Lorenz and two other ethologists—Karl von Frisch of Austria and Nikolaas

Tinbergen, born in the Netherlands—received the 1973 Nobel Prize for physiology or medicine for their work on animal behavior.

Unlike psychologists, who had studied animal behavior in laboratories, Lorenz studied animals in their natural environments. He observed that instinct plays a major role in animal behavior—a view that conflicted with the ideas of many psychologists. He described the instinctive process of *imprinting,* by which, for example, an animal may learn to identify its owner as its parent.

Lorenz was born in Vienna. He earned an M.D. degree in 1928 and a Ph.D. degree in 1933, both at the University of Vienna. In 1954, Lorenz became codirector of the Max Planck Institute for Physiology of Behavior in Germany. He became director of the Institute of Comparative Ethology of the Austrian Academy of Sciences in 1973.

Lorenz wrote several books on animals and their behavior. They include *King Solomon's Ring* (1952) and *On Aggression* (1966).

Macoun, John

John Macoun (1832–1920) was an Irish-born Canadian botanist and naturalist whose explorations of the terrain and vegetation of Canada contributed to the young nation's agricultural and transportation development.

In 1881, Macoun was appointed to the Geological Survey of Canada, serving as botanist, assistant director, and naturalist.

Macoun founded the Dominion Herbarium, contributing to it his personal collection of nearly 100,000 plant specimen sheets.

In 1882, he was made a charter member of the Royal Society of Canada. He wrote *Catalogue of Canadian Plants* (1883–1902), *Catalogue of Canadian Birds* (1900–1904), and other publications. Many species and varieties of organisms are named after Macoun.

Mayr, Ernst Walter

Ernst Walter Mayr *(ehrnst VAHL tuhr myr)* (1904–   ), a German-born American biologist,

made influential contributions to the study of evolution. He helped develop the synthetic theory of evolution. This theory *synthesizes* (combines) evolution theory with genetics and other sciences.

Mayr defined a biological species as a group of living things that breed only with one another. Using this definition, he developed theories for how species *evolve* (gradually change). Mayr argued that living things evolve when a few members of a species become physically isolated from the rest of that species. The isolated population has a specific pool of *genes,* the biochemical substances that carry traits from one generation to the next. Genetic mutation and other factors may cause the isolated group to develop new characteristics and create a new species. According to Mayr, species can isolate themselves by simply wandering off from the main population. Such groups may evolve in a relatively short time. Mayr called this phenomenon *peripatric speciation.*

Mayr was born in Kempten, Germany. In 1926, he received a doctorate in zoology from the University of Berlin. He moved to the United States in 1931 and became a U.S. citizen in 1932. Mayr served as a curator at the American Museum of Natural History and a professor at Harvard University. He wrote several books on the history of evolutionary theory, including *The Growth of Biological Thought* (1982).

Mendel, Gregor Johann

Gregor Johann Mendel *(GREHG uhr YOH hahn MEHN duhl)* (1822–1884), an Austrian botanist and monk, formulated the basic laws of heredity. His experiments with the breeding of garden peas led to the development of the science of genetics.

Mendel was born on July 22, 1822, in Heinzendorf, Austria (now Hyncice, near Krnov, in what is now the Czech Republic). His parents were peasants. In 1843, Mendel entered the monastery of St. Thomas in Brunn, Austria (now Brno, the Czech Republic). He became a priest in 1847. In 1851, the monastery sent Mendel to study science and mathematics at the University of Vienna. He returned to the monastery in 1853 and taught biology and physics at a local high school for the next 14 years. Mendel's fame came from his research in the monastery garden. In 1868, Mendel was elected abbot of the monastery. From then on, his administrative responsibilities limited his opportunities for research.

In his experiments, Mendel studied the inheritance of seven pairs of traits in garden pea plants and in their seeds. These pairs included (1) rounded or wrinkled seeds and (2) tall or short plants.

Mendel bred and crossbred thousands of plants and observed the characteristics of each successive generation. Like all organisms that reproduce sexually, pea plants produce their offspring through the union of special sex cells called *gametes.* In pea plants, a male gamete, or sperm cell, combines with a female gamete, or egg cell, to form a seed.

Mendel concluded that plant traits are handed down through hereditary elements in the gametes. These elements are now called *genes.* He reasoned that each plant receives a pair of genes for each trait, one gene from each of its parents. Based on his experiments, he concluded that if a plant inherits two different genes for a trait, one gene will be *dominant* and the other will be *recessive.* The trait of the dominant gene will appear in the plant. For example, the gene for round seeds is dominant, and the gene for wrinkled seeds is recessive. A plant that inherits both genes will have round seeds.

Mendel also concluded that the pairs of genes *segregate* (separate) in a random fashion when a plant's gametes are formed. Thus, a parent plant hands down only one gene of each pair to its offspring. In addition, Mendel believed that a plant inherits each of its traits independently of other traits. These two conclusions are known as Mendel's *Law of Segregation* and his *Law of Independent Assortment.* Since Mendel's time, scientists have discovered some exceptions to his conclusions, but his theories in general have been proved.

Mendel died on Jan. 6, 1884. His results were published in 1866 but went unnoticed until 1900.

Merriam, Clinton Hart

Clinton Hart Merriam *(MARY uhm)* (1855–1942) was an American physician and zoologist. His expeditions for wildlife study in the western United States led to a compilation of data that helped to define the geographic distribution of animals and plants throughout the country. He later studied the Pacific Coast Indians. He also was a founder of the National Geographic Society in 1888.

In 1872, he joined the Government Survey of the Territories (also known as the Hayden Survey) and collected many birds in Utah, Idaho, and Wyoming.

In 1885, the entomological division of the U.S. Department of Agriculture (which later became the United States Bureau of Biological Survey, now known as the U.S. Fish and Wildlife Service) was established, originally to survey bird distribution in the United States. Merriam served as the bureau's director until 1910 and under his guidance the agency was expanded to also include the study of plants and animals. He also was instrumental in establishing federal responsibility toward wildlife conservation by helping to secure the Lacey Act of 1900, which prohibited interstate commerce in illegally killed game and regulated the importation of foreign species.

In 1899, Merriam organized and directed an expedition to Alaska sponsored by railroad financier Edward H. Harriman. The resulting compilation of the data gathered is of value to conservationists today. Around that time, Merriman developed his "life zones" theory, which stated that temperature patterns determined the geographic distribution of plants and animals.

Mohl, Hugo von

Hugo von Mohl (1855-1942) , a German botanist, helped develop the cell theory. According to this theory, all plants and animals are made up of cells, which divide to form new cells. Mohl gave the name protoplasm to the part of the cell that surrounds the nucleus. He is also known for his work on the microscopic structure of plants. Mohl was born in Stuttgart.

Mohs, Friedrich

Friedrich Mohs (1773–1839) was a German mineralogist who invented the *Mohs scale* for classifying the relative hardness of materials. The hardness of minerals may be tested by scratching one mineral with another. The harder mineral scratches the softer one, and mineralogists use a scale of hardness based on this principle.

The Mohs hardness scale lists 10 minerals from the softest to the hardest, numbered from 1 to 10. The hardness of other minerals is found by determining whether they scratch, or are scratched by, the minerals in the Mohs scale. For example, galena scratches gypsum (number 2), but is scratched by calcite (number 3). Therefore, galena's hardness is 2½ —about halfway between that of gypsum and calcite.

The scale is as follows: talc 1; gypsum 2; calcite 3; fluorite 4; apatite 5; feldspar 6; quartz 7; topaz 8; corundum 9; diamond 10. A human fingernail measures 2+ on the scale; a copper coin about 3; and a pocketknife blade about 5+. As certain substances may only *appear* to be scratched when in contact with others, care must be taken to ensure that the apparent "scratch" is not just a mark which can be rubbed off.

Friedrich Mohs was born on Jan. 29, 1773, in Gernrode, near Quedlinburg, and was educated at the University of Halle. He was a professor at the universities of Graz and Vienna, both in Austria, and Freiburg, Germany. His written works include *The Natural History System of Mineralogy* (1821) and *Treatise on Mineralogy* (1825). Mohs died on Sept. 29, 1839, in Agordo, Italy, near Belluno.

Molloy, Georgiana

Georgiana Molloy (1805–1843) was a botanist and a member of a pioneering family in Western Australia.

Georgiana Kennedy was born on May 23, 1805, in Cumberland, England. In 1831, she married Captain John Molloy, a veteran of the Napoleonic Wars. Shortly afterward, the couple sailed for Western Australia and established themselves at Augusta, south of Bunbury.

Georgiana Molloy developed an interest in collecting botanical specimens. She carefully packed and labeled seeds, leaves, and flowers. English botanists were deeply interested in Western Australia's strange and unknown wildflowers. Molloy sent her collections to a well-known English botanist, Captain James Mangles of the Royal Navy, who distributed them among English public gardens and parks. Over the years, Molloy's botanical collections became large, particularly when the family moved northward to the Vasse River. In return, Mangles forwarded English seeds for her garden and botanical books. The books greatly assisted Molloy in classifying her plants, as well as extending her knowledge of Western Australian plants. She also collected specimens for a visiting German botanist, Ludwig Preiss. Molloy died on April 8, 1843, soon after giving birth to her sixth child.

Morris, Desmond

Desmond Morris (1928–   ) is a British zoologist. He has written or co-written more than a dozen books that have increased popular interest in the behavior of animals and human beings. Morris has also helped make films and television programs that explore the social behavior of animals.

Morris's best-known books are *The Naked Ape* (1967) and *The Human Zoo* (1969). These books, written from the viewpoint of a zoologist, discuss the basic elements of animal behavior in human beings. Morris examines the ways that humans behave socially in modern-day urban society. *The Naked Ape* became widely popular, but some scientists criticized it because they thought its entertainment value outweighed its scientific value. Morris also wrote *The Biology of Art* (1962) and *The Mammals: A Guide to the Living Species* (1965). With his wife, Ramona Morris, he wrote *Men and Snakes* (1965), *Men and Apes* (1966), and *Men and Pandas* (1966). Desmond John Morris was born in Purton, England, near Swindon.

Muir, John

John Muir *(myoor)* (1838–1914), an explorer, naturalist, and writer, campaigned for the conservation of land, water, and forests in the United States. His efforts influenced Congress to pass the Yosemite National Park Bill in 1890, establishing both Yosemite and Sequoia national parks. Muir helped persuade President Theodore Roosevelt to set aside 148 million acres (59,900,000 hectares) of forest reserves. A redwood forest near San Francisco was named Muir Woods in 1908 in his honor.

Muir tramped through many regions of the United States, Europe, Asia, Africa, and the Arctic. He spent six years in the area of Yosemite Valley and was the first person to explain the valley's glacial origin. In 1879, Muir discovered a glacier in Alaska that now bears his name. He called California "the grand side of the mountain" and owned a large fruit ranch there. In 1892, he founded the Sierra Club, which became a leading conservation organization. Muir wrote a number of books, including *The Mountains of California* (1894), *Our National Parks* (1901), and *The Yosemite* (1912).

Muir was born in Dunbar, Scotland. His family moved to Wisconsin when he was 11. He grew up on a farm and developed a great love of nature. As a boy, he attracted attention with his inventions. He entered the University of Wisconsin at the age of 22. Muir supported himself by teaching and by doing farm work during the summer. His interests included botany and geology.

Murray, John

John Murray (1841–1914) was a British naturalist, oceanographer, and deep-sea explorer. He specialized in studying the ocean bottom. He was one of the naturalists on the expedition of H.M.S. *Challenger,* which made a scientific study of oceans and ocean bottoms from 1872 to 1876. Afterward, Murray edited the expedition's 50 volumes of scientific reports. He also wrote *The Depths of the Ocean* (1912) and *The Ocean* (1913), considered a classic in its field. Murray was

born in Cobourg, Ontario. He graduated from the University of Edinburgh. He made a notable study of Scottish *lochs* (lakes).

Nägeli, Karl Wilhelm

Karl Wilhelm Nägeli *(NA guh lee)* (1817–1891), a Swiss botanist and philosopher, studied the growth of roots, stems, and pollen grains. He discovered the nitrogenous nature of protoplasm, and he described cell division in the formation of pollen and in simple algae. His philosophical views led him to scorn Gregor Mendel's proof of heredity.

Nägeli was born in Kilchberg, Switzerland. He was professor of botany at the universities of Freiburg, Zurich, and Munich.

Nice, Margaret Morse

Margaret Morse Nice (1883–1974), an American ornithologist, became one of the world's foremost bird behaviorists by adapting the techniques of psychology to the study of bird behavior.

Together with her husband, Leonard Nice, she wrote the first complete study of the birds of Oklahoma (1924). Using colored bands to identify individual song sparrows by name and number, Nice was able to track their behavior and outline their life history in greater detail than had ever before been attempted. Her two-part *Studies in the Life History of the Song Sparrow* (1937, 1943) established her reputation as an extraordinary scholar.

There were fewer opportunities to observe and collect data about birds in Chicago, where the Nices moved in 1936 when Leonard Nice was appointed to the faculty of the Chicago Medical School. Using data from earlier observations, however, Margaret continued to publish for the next 30 years. She also spoke out about ecological issues, remained involved in ornithological and conservation organizations, and published reviews of European research of interest to bird lovers.

Owen, Richard

Richard Owen (1804–1892), a British anatomist and paleontologist, gave the name *Dinosauria* (terrible lizards) to the large, extinct reptiles whose remains began to be discovered in the 1800's.

As superintendent of the natural history departments of the British Museum (1856–1884), Owen oversaw the building of the Natural History Museum in South Kensington. He also served as Fullerian Professor of Physiology at the Royal Institution (1859–1861).

Owen wrote over 360 scholarly monographs. His work on invertebrates included an 1835 paper describing the parasite that causes trichinosis. He also published many anatomical accounts of various primates. His interest in fossils resulted from a friendship with Charles Darwin, who asked Owen to describe the fossils he brought back on the H.M.S. *Beagle*. Although Owen never accepted Darwinian evolution, his four-volume *History of British Fossil Reptiles* (1849–1884) was a model of painstaking scholarship. After examining reptilelike fossil bones found in southern England, he suggested that the bones were from creatures belonging to a group of reptiles unlike any living creature. In 1842, he called this group *Dinosauria*. Its members later became known as dinosaurs.

Peterson, Roger Tory

Roger Tory Peterson (1908–1996) was an American artist, naturalist, and author. His popular paintings and illustrations of birds for books led to the development of a series of nature handbooks called the *Peterson Field Guide Series*. His work has helped people identify and appreciate animals in their natural environment and has highlighted the value of wildlife conservation.

Peterson first collected his illustrations and methods of identifying birds in a book called *Field Guide to the Birds* (1934). Later, he created *A Field Guide to Western Birds* (1941). In 1946, he became editor of the *Peterson Field Guide Series*. Peterson expanded the series to include guides on birds of Europe and Mexico, on other animals, on plants, and on minerals.

Peterson was born in Jamestown, New York. His books include *Birds Over America* (1948), *The Birds* (1963), and *Penguins* (1979). With James Fisher, a naturalist, Peterson wrote *Wild America* (1955) and *The World of Birds* (1964). In 1986, Peterson and several colleagues founded the Roger Tory Peterson Institute of Natural History in Jamestown.

Ray, John

John Ray (1627–1705), a British naturalist, is regarded as the founder of systematic zoology. From 1662 to 1666, he traveled throughout western Europe with a pupil named Francis Willughby. Together they collected various specimens and attempted to classify them. At first, Ray classified plant life and Willughby classified animal life. But, after Willughby died, Ray continued Willughby's work on animal life. Ray was born in Black Notley, in the county of Essex, England.

His pioneering works were *Catalogus Plantarum Angliae* (1670), *Methodus Plantarum Nova* (1682), and *Historia Plantarum* (3 volumes, 1686–1704). In *The Wisdom of God Manifested in the Works of the Creation* (1691), Ray discussed the adaptation of organisms to their environment.

Ray based his classifications on accurate observation and identification. He rejected the mythological material that was common in works of botany and zoology. His classification set the stage for Carolus Linnaeus, the Swedish naturalist and botanist, who established the modern scientific method of naming plants and animals in the 1700's.

The Ray Society was founded in 1844 and named in honor of Ray. It publishes academic works that are of interest to naturalists, zoologists, botanists, and collectors.

Sachs, Julius von

Julius von Sachs *(zahks)* (1832–1897), a German botanist, was the founder of the science of plant physiology. His *Textbook of Botany* (1868) had great influence in the United States by emphasizing the use of living plants in teaching botany. His *History of Botany* (1875) is one of the best sources of information about all aspects of botany up to 1860. Sachs was born in Breslau, Germany (now Wroclaw, Poland).

Schaller, George Beals

George Beals Schaller *(SHAH luhr)* (1933–   ) is an American zoologist known for his writings on endangered species of animals. He has studied and photographed animals in many parts of the world.

Schaller is best known for his studies of large mammals. He has observed the behavior of lions in Tanzania, mountain gorillas in Zaire—now Congo (Kinshasa)—and Uganda, tigers in India, and giant pandas in China. He also studied white pelicans in Wyoming, caribou in Alaska, and sea otters in California. He watched the animals daily as they hunted, ate, and cared for their young.

Schaller's studies have provided valuable information on the conditions needed for the survival of endangered species. This information can be used in planning programs to protect the animals' environment.

Schaller has written many books and articles on animal behavior. His book *The Serengeti Lion: A Study of Predator-Prey Relations* (1972) was awarded the 1973 National Book Award for the sciences. Schaller's other books include *The Year of the Gorilla* (1964), *Stones of Silence: Journeys in the Himalaya* (1980), *The Giant Pandas of Wolong* (1985), and *The Last Panda* (1993).

Schaller was born on May 26, 1933, in Berlin, Germany. He graduated from the University of Alaska in 1955 and earned a Ph.D. degree at the University of Wisconsin in 1962. In 1972, Schaller became a zoologist at the New York Zoological Society. In 1988, he became science director at the society, which is now called the Wildlife Conservation Society.

Schleiden, Matthias

Matthias Schleiden (1804–1881) was a German *botanist,* a scientist who studies plants. Schleiden was the first to recognize the importance of cells as the fundamental units of living organisms (the cell theory) when, in 1838, he announced that the various parts of plants consist of cells or derivatives of cells.

While attending the University of Berlin, he met Theodor Schwann, a German *physiologist* (scientist who studies how living things function). In a scientific paper published in 1838, Schleiden stated that the cell was the basic unit of all life. Schleiden's research involved plants, but Schwann believed that the same idea also applied to animals. Schwann advanced the cell theory in a paper published in 1839.

Schleiden also wrote a number of popular books on biology and history.

Scott, Peter

Peter Scott (1909–1989), a British artist and ornithologist, became well known for his paintings of birds and for his television broadcasts on conservation and wildlife. As an ornithologist, he founded the Wildfowl Trust in Slimbridge, Gloucestershire, and led expeditions to many parts of the world. As a yachtsman, he represented the United Kingdom in the Olympic Games and the America's Cup race. In 1963, he won the national gliding championship. Scott was chairman of the World Wildlife Fund (now the World Wide Fund for Nature). His books include *Portrait Drawings* (1949), *Wildfowl of the British Isles* (1957), and *The Eye of the Wind* (1961), his autobiography.

Peter Markham Scott was born in London on Sept. 14, 1909. His father was Robert Falcon Scott, the Antarctic explorer. Peter Scott was knighted in 1973 and died on Aug. 29, 1989.

Sears, Paul Bigelow

Paul Bigelow Sears (1891–1990), an American botanist, was an authority on pollens, applied ecology, and the historical study of vegetation patterns. He was also an important popularizer of science. Sears headed the botany departments at the University of Oklahoma and Oberlin College. He became chairman of the Yale University conservation program in 1950. His books include

Deserts on the March (1935), *This Is Our World* (1937), and *The Living Landscape* (1966).

Sereno, Paul C.

Paul C. Sereno (1957–) is an American paleontologist who has made a number of major dinosaur discoveries. His success resulted in part from his boldness in venturing to remote regions where travel is difficult both physically and politically.

Sereno made his first expedition to Lord Howe Island, Australia, in 1980. In 1984, he became the first American graduate student of paleontology to study in China. Sereno then became the first paleontologist to work in the Gobi Desert after Mongolia had excluded foreigners decades earlier.

In 1988, on his first expedition to Argentina, he searched the Ischigualasto region, an area with sediments dating from 225 million years ago, when dinosaurs were thought to have first lived. Sereno found the most complete and well-preserved skeleton of a *Herrerasaurus,* one of the earliest meat-eating dinosaurs.

In 1991, Sereno discovered *Eoraptor* (dawn raptor), one of the earliest known dinosaurs, near where he found *Herrerasaurus.* The meat-eating *Eoraptor* lived about 228 million years ago, and scientists believe *Eoraptor* may resemble the common ancestor of all dinosaurs. *Eoraptor* was about 3 feet (90 centimeters) long and ran upright on its hind legs.

Sereno turned his attention to Africa, which was then an unexplored area for dinosaurs. He made expeditions to Niger in 1993 and 1997 and to Morocco in 1995.

In Niger, Sereno found the bones of *Afrovenator* (African hunter), a predator 27 feet (8 meters) long. He and his helpers also found a *sauropod* 60 feet (18 meters) long, which he named *Jobaria.* They also found *Suchomimus,* a fin-backed fish-eater 36 feet (11 meters) long.

In Morocco, Sereno's expedition discovered *Deltadromeus* (delta runner), a fast predator 27 feet (8 meters) long, in 90-million-year-old rocks. They also discovered the large skull of the predator *Carcharodontosaurus* (shark-toothed reptile) in the same area. One of the largest meat-eating dinosaurs ever found, it measured 45 feet (14 meters) long, as large as *Tyrannosaurus rex.*

Sereno has studied and written on the origin and evolution of dinosaurs. He works to teach young people to enjoy science. He has helped make documentary films on dinosaurs and has written about his expeditions for *National Geographic* and other magazines.

Simpson, George Gaylord

George Gaylord Simpson (1902–1984), was an American paleontologist who helped advance the study of evolution. He led several expeditions that found numerous prehistoric animal fossils. His studies of these and other fossils led him to make refinements to evolutionary theory.

In his book *Tempo and Mode in Evolution* (1944), Simpson argued that living things *evolve* (gradually change) in three ways. He labeled these ways *speciation, phyletic evolution,* and *quantum evolution.* In speciation, individual members of a species leave the main population and evolve into a new species. In phyletic evolution, an entire species slowly evolves into a new species. In quantum evolution, isolated members of a species evolve rapidly into a new species. Simpson's ideas led to the development of the *synthetic theory of evolution.* This theory *synthesizes* (combines) evolution theory with paleontology and other sciences.

Simpson was born in Chicago. In 1926, he received his doctoral degree from Yale University. Simpson served as curator of vertebrate fossils at the American Museum of Natural History. He was also a professor of paleontology at Harvard University.

Sloane, Hans

Hans Sloane (1660–1753) was a British physician and botanist renowned especially for his voluminous collection of plant and animal specimens, fossils, minerals, precious stones, coins, and rare artifacts and antiquities of all kinds. That collection inspired the founding of the British Museum in 1753.

He wrote *Catalogus Plantarum* (1696) and a two-volume set on the natural history of Jamaica (1707–1725), which became a classic. His writings were used by Carolus Linnaeus in developing his own major work, the *Species Plantarum.* Over time, Sloane's collection grew significantly, establishing it as one of the greatest and most extensive collections of its time.

Because Sloane wished his collection to benefit the public, he willed it to the British nation, and after his death, Parliament established the British Museum to house it and his library of over 50,000 books. The collection became the core of the British Museum and later the Natural History Museum.

Smith, James Leonard Brierley

James Leonard Brierley Smith (1897–1968), a South African expert on fish, was the first person to identify the coelacanth as a living species. The *coelacanth* is a primitive fish that first lived more than 300 million years ago. Scientists believed it was extinct until a specimen was caught in 1938.

Smith was born in Graaff-Reinet, the Cape Colony (now the Eastern Cape province of South Africa). In 1923, he became a lecturer in chemistry at Rhodes University, Grahamstown. Smith's passion for fishing led him to devise a unique system of fish classification. In January 1939, the curator of the East London Museum, Marjorie Courtenay Latimer, sent him a sketch of a strange fish and asked him to identify it. It had been netted the previous year off the southeast coast of South Africa. Smith was convinced that it was a coelacanth and classified it scientifically as *Latimeria chalumnae.* Several expeditions looked for a second specimen, and one was caught in 1952. Since then, several more specimens have been caught. At Rhodes, Smith was honored by being appointed the first professor of *ichthyology* (study of fishes) in South Africa. He died on Jan. 7, 1968.

Smith, John Maynard

John Maynard Smith (1920–   ) is a world-renowned British evolutionary biologist and author of numerous books on evolution, both scientific and popular. He is acclaimed for his study of the parallels between game theory and the evolutionary "strategies" that occur at a biological level to maintain a species' existence.

One of Smith's enduring interests as an evolutionary biologist has been studying the ways in which an organism utilizes information in order to evolve, and how this information at times results in major evolutionary transition points in an organism or species. In 1982, he published the groundbreaking *Evolution and the Theory of Games,* in which he applied game theory to the process of evolutionary selection. Game theory, developed in the 1940's by John von Neumann, has shown that in games such as chess or poker, the optimal strategy for winning may change, depending on the actions of the opponent.

Smith found a similar "evolutionary stable strategy" occurring in nature, in that natural selection of characteristics within a population of competing species is guided by the impulse for balance, thus optimizing the chances for survival of each species.

Smith, William

William Smith (1769–1839), an English geologist and engineer, was the first scientist to use fossils to identify and also determine the relative age of rock *strata* (layers). Smith discovered in the late 1700's that each layer of rock contained its own characteristic fossils. He noticed that the fossils in the various layers were arranged in chronological sequence. Thus, Smith could tell the age of strata in relation to one another. He also noted that fossils in any layer change little from place to place. Therefore, Smith could trace and compare the strata of widely separated areas.

Smith used fossils to draw a geological map of England that showed strata of different ages underlying the entire country. This map was one of the first attempts to show the relation between rock formations in any large area. Today, geologists use fossils as a primary means of identifying rock strata.

Solander, Daniel Charles

Daniel Charles Solander (1733–1782) was a Swedish naturalist. The English naturalist Sir Joseph Banks hired Solander in 1768 as a scientific assistant on the English navigator James Cook's first voyage of exploration. During that voyage, Solander helped Banks collect and classify more than 1,000 species of plants that had previously been unknown in Europe. Solander became Banks's secretary and librarian, and worked with him on several natural history projects.

Solander was born on Feb. 19, 1733, in Norrland, Sweden. He studied under the Swedish naturalist Carolus Linnaeus at the University of Uppsala before traveling to Britain in 1760. He worked for some years at the British Museum and, in 1764, was elected a fellow of the Royal Society, one of the world's foremost scientific organizations. Solander died on May 13, 1782.

Steno, Nicolaus

Nicolaus Steno (1638–1686) was a Danish anatomist and geologist whose work provided a deeper understanding of anatomy, geology, paleontology, and crystallography. He proposed a scientific explanation for fossils and geological strata long before geology was recognized as a legitimate science.

Steno was born Niels Stensen in Copenhagen, Denmark, but is better known by the Latinized form of his name, Nicolaus Steno. Settling in Tuscany in 1666, Steno served as house physician to Grand Duke Ferdinand II of Tuscany. Over the next 10 years, he published several important treatises detailing his findings in both anatomy and geology. He was ordained as a priest in 1675 and, after becoming a bishop in 1677, abandoned science to spend the rest of his life serving his faith.

As a geologist he recognized, as did a few of his contemporaries, that fossils had once been living organisms that were petrified after death, and his work with fossils led him to try to understand the more general question of how any solid object (for example, a fossil) could come to be found inside another solid object, such as a rock or a layer of rock. Steno reasoned that rock strata and similar deposits were generally formed in horizontal layers. This reasoning led to his most important contribution to geology: Steno's law of superposition. It states that the earth's strata are layered, with the oldest layer on the bottom and the youngest layer at the top, unless later processes disturbed this arrangement. Thus, he was essentially the first to identify the evolution of the earth over time by means of geology.

Suess, Eduard

Eduard Suess (*zyoos*) (1831–1914), an Austrian geologist, became famous for his work on changes of the earth's surface. His most important book was the four-volume *Face of the Earth* (1885–1901). He served as an assistant at the Hofmuseum in Vienna from 1852 to 1862, and taught at the University of Vienna from 1857 to 1901. From 1869 to 1896, he served as leader of the Liberal Party in the Austrian Parliament. Suess was born in London.

Swammerdam, Jan

Jan Swammerdam (*yahn SVAHM uhr DAHM*) (1637–1680) was a Dutch anatomist and zoologist. He pioneered in the use of the microscope to study minute structures within animals. He was the first to observe red blood cells.

Swammerdam's observations on the life history, anatomy, and development of insects led to a system of insect classification that is still considered useful. This system is based on the different patterns of *metamorphosis* found in various types of insects. Metamorphosis is the change in form that many insects undergo to become adults. Swammerdam also made important observations on how nerves and muscles function.

Swammerdam was born in Amsterdam, the Netherlands. He studied medicine before beginning his anatomical research.

Theophrastus

Theophrastus (ca. 372 B.C.–ca. 287 B.C.) was a Greek botanist, mineralogist, and philosopher whose classification methods laid the foundation for modern botany. His botanical works are the first detailed, generally accurate treatment of their kind in world literature, and he is known as the "father of botany."

Theophrastus studied in Athens, at first with Plato and then with Aristotle, and became Aristotle's favorite student and good friend. When Aristotle retired around 322 B.C., Theophrastus assumed the leadership of his Lyceum, or school. The school, known as the *Peripatetic school,* achieved its highest enrollment in the 35 years under Theophrastus's guidance, with more than 2,000 students.

He continued with Aristotle's teachings and expanded upon some of them. He wrote more than 200 works on science, philosophy, history, law, literature, music, poetry, and politics. Most notable are *De Historia Plantarum (Enquiry into Plants),* which describes, examines, and classifies trees and plants, and *De Causis Plantarum (Etiology of Plants),* which deals with origin, propagation, and cultivation. In these books, Theophrastus evaluated about 550 species and varieties of plants from the Atlantic through the Mediterranean region and as far east as India. His sources of information included men who accompanied Alexander the Great on his campaigns. He also relied on technical writings by other contemporary scientists.

Theophrastus noted that plants could not be generalized as a whole because no one thing was common to all of them. He classified them in groups according to shared characteristics, such as trunks, bark, leaves, seeds, and flowers. He also examined plant propagation and growth, odor and taste, the effects of weather and the environment, and the origin and propagation of cereals.

His book *De Lapidibus,* the first methodical study of mineralogy, described his theories on the formation of minerals and metals. He believed that their solidification was due sometimes to heat and other times to cold. He classified a wide range of stones and mineral earths, describing their tactile qualities and behavior.

Thompson, D'Arcy Wentworth

D'Arcy Wentworth Thompson (1860–1948) was a Scottish zoologist who combined natural history and mathematics to develop a new approach to evolution and the growth of living things. His work has been a great contribution to embryology, taxonomy, paleontology, and ecology.

Thompson was born in Edinburgh, Scotland, in 1860. In the early 1900's, Thompson revolutionized the science of natural history by applying mathematics and physics to explain biological phenomena. In his book *On Growth and Form* (1917), he examined the development of form and structure in living things and how physical forces affect them. He noted how such things as the six-sided shape of cells in a bee honeycomb, the curve of a snail shell, and the spiral arrangement of seeds in a sunflower all follow mathematical principles. He also demonstrated how the trabeculae, or lattice-work, of calcium deposition in bone is aligned to most efficiently cope with the stresses placed on the bone. He illustrated this by comparing the metal cross structures of a hoisting crane with the internal structure of a femur.

Tinbergen, Nikolaas

Nikolaas Tinbergen (1907–1988), a Dutch-born zoologist, studied how the behavior of animals is adapted to their environment. He also investigated the evolution of animal behavior over time by comparing behavior patterns in various species. Tinbergen shared the 1973 Nobel Prize in physiology or medicine with Austrian naturalists Konrad Lorenz and Karl von Frisch. They received the award for their studies of animal behavior.

Tinbergen worked with birds, butterflies, fish, wasps, and other animals in their natural surroundings. His best-known research concerns the social behavior of gulls. Tinbergen also applied ideas about animal behavior to the behavior of children suffering from a developmental disorder called autism.

Tinbergen, the brother of economist Jan Tinbergen, was born in The Hague. He earned a doctorate from Leiden University in 1932. Tinbergen served on the faculty of Oxford University in England from 1949 until his death. His books include *The Study of Instinct* (1951), *The Herring Gull's World* (1953), and *The Animal in Its World* (1972, 1973). He was coauthor of *Autistic Children: New Hope for a Cure* (1983).

Tyrrell, Joseph Burr

Joseph Burr Tyrrell *(TIHR ehl)* (1858–1957) was a Canadian geologist, naturalist, and explorer whose work led to much of what is known about the western and northern regions of Canada. His surveys greatly impacted coal and gold mining in Canada, and he also made a significant discovery of dinosaur remains there.

Tyrrell was born in Ontario, Canada, in 1858. He studied chemistry, biology, mineralogy, and geology at the University of Toronto. He took a job as a field assistant with the Geological Survey of Canada, and in 1883 he surveyed and mapped the area of the Crows Nest, Kootenay, and Kicking Horse passes in the Canadian Rocky Mountains.

In 1884, Tyrrell began a geological survey of the Cretaceous coal and mineral deposits in the foothills of Alberta between Calgary and Edmonton. On June 9, 1884, while examining exposed rocks in the Drumheller region, he discovered the remains of a dinosaur, the first discovery of its kind in Canada. In his field notes, he wrote that he had found a "large and fairly perfect head of a gigantic carnivore." In fact, the partial skull belonged to a new genus of dinosaur that later was called *Albertosaurus*. Three days later, on June 12, he discovered one of Canada's largest coal deposits nearby.

Tyrrell also provided a detailed catalogue of Canadian mammals, descriptions of winter homes of the caribou, and a description of conifers and their distribution.

Van Hise, Charles Richard

Charles Richard van Hise *(van HYS)* (1857–1918) was an American geologist and educator. He was a member of the United States Geological Survey from 1883 to 1900, specializing in ancient rocks of the Lake Superior region. From 1903 to 1918, he served as president of the University of Wisconsin. His book, *Conservation of Natural Resources in the United States* (1910), was important in this field. Van Hise was born in Fulton, Wisconsin. He taught geology at the University of Wisconsin and at the University of Chicago.

Von Frisch, Karl

Karl von Frisch (1886–1982), an Austrian zoologist, was a pioneer in the field of animal behavior. Frisch and two naturalists—Konrad Lorenz of Austria and Nikolaas Tinbergen, who was born in the Netherlands—won the 1973 Nobel Prize in physiology or medicine.

Frisch's best-known work dealt with the communication system of bees. He discovered that bees "dance" in certain patterns to tell members of their hive where to find food. These patterns can indicate the distance and direction of food from the hive. Frisch also showed that fish can see colors. Scientists had previously thought fish were color blind.

Frisch was born in Vienna. He studied at the Universities of Munich and Vienna and received a Ph.D. degree from the latter institution in 1910. From 1910 to 1958, he taught at several European universities. Frisch wrote many books, including *Bees: Their Vision, Chemical Senses, and Language* (1971), and *A Biologist Remembers* (1967), an autobiography.

Von Mueller, Baron Ferdinand

Baron Ferdinand von Mueller (1825–1896) was a German-born Australian botanist who made extensive contributions to the knowledge of native Australian plants. He was the first government botanist of Victoria, Australia, and began a botanical collection that grew to become Australia's national herbarium.

Ferdinand Jakob Heinrich von Mueller was born in Rostock, Mecklenburg-Schwerin (now in Germany) in 1825. He received a Ph.D. degree in botany from the University of Kiel in Germany. Out of health concerns, von Mueller sailed for the warm climate of Australia in 1847. At the time von Mueller arrived there, little was known about Australian plant life. He immediately proved himself a skilled botanist and rose quickly in his career. He made numerous trips to the interior, collecting plants of all kinds, and wrote about his findings in a lifelong series of books and papers.

In 1853, after moving to neighboring Victoria, he was appointed the first government botanist there, a position he held until the end of his life. Von Mueller also served as director of the Melbourne Botanic Gardens from 1857 through 1873 and as botanist on the North West Australian Expedition from 1855 through 1856. The scientific designation of hundreds of Australian plants now reference von Mueller's name.

Wallace, Alfred Russel

Alfred Russel Wallace (1823–1913) was a British naturalist and explorer. He independently developed the same principle of *natural selection* as did British naturalist Charles Darwin. Natural selection is a process by which historical changes occur in species of plants and animals. The changes occur because of higher survival rates of individuals with hereditary traits that make them better suited to their environment. This process is the basis of evolution. Wallace also established the principles of *animal geography*—the study of the geographical distribution of animal species.

From 1848 to 1852, Wallace explored the Amazon Basin with British naturalist Henry Walter Bates. Wallace traveled to the East Indies in 1854 and remained there eight years collecting data. He found that the mammals of the Malay Archipelago are divided by an imaginary line into two groups of species. This line became known as *Wallace's Line.* Species west of the line are more closely related to

mammals of Asia, and those east of the line are closer relatives of mammals of Australia.

Wallace was born on Jan. 8, 1823, in Usk, Wales. He wrote *The Malay Archipelago* (1869) and *Geographical Distribution of Animals* (1876). He died on Nov. 7, 1913.

Werner, Abraham Gottlob

Abraham Gottlob Werner *(AH brah hahm GOHT lohp VEHR nur)* (1749–1817), a German geologist, formulated a theory on the origin of Earth that was widely accepted in his time. Werner believed all rocks of Earth were formed from a giant ocean. Scientists accepted this theory for years until it was proved that some rocks were formed by the cooling of hot lava from volcanoes. Werner also introduced a system of identifying and classifying rocks and created new methods of describing minerals.

Werner was born on Sept. 25, 1749, in Wehrau, Saxony. He taught at the Freiberg School of Mines in Freiberg from 1775 until his death on June 30, 1817. Students came from throughout Europe to hear Werner explain complex ideas in a simple way. His lectures helped geology gain respect as an important area of study.

White, Gilbert

Gilbert White (1720–1793), an English naturalist, wrote *Natural History and Antiquities of Selborne* (1789), a work considered a classic by naturalists and students of English literature. It is based on letters written by White to two naturalists, Thomas Pennant and Daines Barrington. Extracts from White's diaries were published as *A Naturalist's Calendar* in 1795.

White was born in Selborne, Hampshire, on July 18, 1720. He died on June 26, 1793. The Selborne Society for the preservation of birds and plants was founded in memory of White in 1885. His house in Selborne was opened to the public as a museum and library in 1955.

Wilson, Edward Osborne

Edward Osborne Wilson (1929–) is an American biologist known for his contributions to the study of animal societies. Wilson helped found the field of *sociobiology,* which studies the biological basis for the social behavior of animals. He argued that *genes* (hereditary material) heavily influence how species behave. Wilson made extensive studies of the social behavior of ants. He observed ant populations worldwide, discovering hundreds of new species. His work with ants also led him to learn how geography, or natural surroundings, plays a role in the formation of species. These and other findings by Wilson helped advance *biogeography,* the science of the distribution of living things.

Wilson was born on June 10, 1929, in Birmingham, Alabama. He received his Ph.D. degree from Harvard University in 1955. After spending one year studying ants in the tropics, Wilson joined the faculty at Harvard in 1956, becoming a full professor there in 1964. He has since held various teaching and research posts at Harvard and its Museum of Comparative Zoology.

Wilson's many books include *The Theory of Island Biogeography* (1967), written with the American ecologist Robert H. MacArthur, as well as *Sociobiology: The New Synthesis* (1975), *The Diversity of Life* (1992), *The Future of Life* (2002), and his autobiography, *Naturalist* (1994). Two of his works won the Pulitzer Prize for general nonfiction: *On Human Nature* (1978) and *The Ants* (1990), which he wrote with the German biologist Bert Holldobler.

Wolberg, Donald Lester

Donald Lester Wolberg (1949–) is an American paleontologist who has made important discoveries and promoted knowledge of paleontology to the public.

Wolberg was born in 1949 in the Bronx, in New York City. He studied geology at New York University and received a Ph.D. degree in geology from the University of Minnesota.

Wolberg worked with federal agencies in the development and funding of scientific and environmental projects. From 1978 to 1994, he served as paleontologist with the New Mexico Bureau of Mines and Mineral Resources. Wolberg was the first to report dinosaur tracks in the San Juan Basin in New Mexico.

Also in New Mexico, Wolberg described a number of new Cretaceous mammals. He launched studies of dinosaurs in southern New Mexico that led to the discovery of *Tyrannosaurus rex* at Elephant Butte.

Wolberg studied fossils from many parts of the world, including South Africa, Greece, China, and Mongolia. In the United States, he worked with fossils in more than 10 states.

Wolberg has received national awards from the U.S. Bureau of Land Management, the American Federation of Mineralogical Societies, and the Paleontological Society. He was secretary of the Paleontological Society from 1988 to 1994.

Wolberg co-wrote *Collecting the Natural World* (1997), a book explaining laws and regulations related to collecting plants, animals, rocks, minerals, and fossils.

Worrell, Eric

Eric Worrell (1924–1987), an Australian naturalist, established the Australian Reptile Park in Gosford, New South Wales, Australia, in 1960. The park houses Australia's largest collection of native reptiles. Many of the poisonous snakes housed at the park are regularly *milked* (have their venom extracted) and the venom is sent to the Commonwealth Serum Laboratories. The venom is used in the manufacture of *antivenins*—that is, antidotes for treating poisonous snakebites. Worrell's books include *Dangerous Snakes of Australia and New Guinea* (1952) and *Reptiles of Australia* (1963). He was born in Sydney.

Additional Resources

Here are some books that will help you further explore the subjects covered in the individual field guides in *World Book's Science & Nature Guides* series. You can also find additional books and magazines at your school library or your local public library.

Amphibians & Reptiles

Encyclopedia of Reptiles and Amphibians Harold G. Cogger and R.G. Zweifel (Academic Press, 1998).

A Field Guide to Reptiles & Amphibians: Eastern and Central North America Roger Conant and J.T. Collins (Houghton Mifflin, 1998).

A Field Guide to Western Reptiles and Amphibians Robert C. Stebbins (Houghton Mifflin, 2003).

Grzimek's Animal Life Encyclopedia: Vol. 6, Amphibians; Vol. 7, Reptiles Bernhard Grzimek (Gale Group, 2003).

National Audubon Society Field Guide to North American Reptiles and Amphibians John L. Behler and F. Wayne King (Knopf, 2000).

National Audubon Society First Field Guide: Reptiles John L. Behler (Scholastic, 1999).

The World's Most Spectacular Reptiles & Amphibians William Lamar (World Publications, 1997).

Birds

Backyard Birds Roger Tory Peterson, editor (Houghton Mifflin, 1996).

Backyard Birds of Summer Carol Lerner (Morrow, 1996) and *Backyard Birds of Winter* (1994).

Birds in Your Backyard Barbara Herkert (Dawn Publications, 2001).

Birds of North America Noel Grove (Hugh Lauter Levin, 1996).

Lives of North American Birds Kenn Kaufman (Houghton Mifflin, 1996) and *Birds of North America* (2000).

National Audubon Society First Field Guide: Birds Scott Weidensaul (Scholastic, 1998).

The Sibley Guide to Birds David Allen Sibley (Knopf, 2000) and *Birding Basics* (2002).

Butterflies

Butterflies and Moths David A. Carter (Dorling Kindersley, 2002).

Butterflies in the Garden Carol Lerner (HarperCollins, 2002).

Butterflies of North America Jim P. Brock and Kenn Kaufman (Houghton Mifflin, 2003).

The Butterflies of North America: A Natural History and Field Guide James A. Scott (Stanford, 1997).

Butterflies Through Binoculars: A Field Guide to the Butterflies of Eastern North America Jeffrey Glassberg (Oxford, 1999) and *Butterflies Through Binoculars: A Field Guide to the Butterflies of Western North America* (2001).

A Field Guide to Eastern Butterflies Paul A. Opler (Houghton Mifflin, 1998) and *A Field Guide to Western Butterflies* (1998).

National Audubon Society Field Guide to Butterflies Robert M. Pyle (Knopf, 2000).

Fossils

Audubon Society Field Guide to North American Fossils Ida Thompson (Knopf, 1982).

Collecting Fossils Steve and Jane Parker (Sterling Publications, 1997).

Fossils Cyril Walker and David Ward (Dorling Kindersley, 2002).

Outside and Inside Dinosaurs Sandra Markle (Atheneum, 2000).

Freshwater Life

The Encyclopedia of Aquatic Life Keith Banister and Andrew Campbell (Facts on File, 1985).

A Field Guide to Freshwater Fishes Lawrence M. Page and Brooks M. Burr (Houghton Mifflin, 1991).

Fresh-Water Invertebrates of the United States Robert W. Pennak (Wiley, 1978).

National Audubon Society Field Guide to Fishes: North America Carter Rowell Gilbert and James D. Williams (Knopf, 2002).

Snakes: The Evolution of Mystery in Nature Harry W. Greene (University of California Press, 1997).

Insects

Bugs: A Close-Up View of the Insect World Christopher Maynard (Dorling Kindersley, 2001).

Bugs A–Z: An A to Z of Insects and Creepy Crawlies Jill Bailey (Blackbirch Press, 2002).

Classifying Insects Andrew Solway (Heinemann Library, 2003).

Firefly Encyclopedia of Insects and Spiders Christopher O'Toole, editor (Firefly Books, 2002).

The Insect Book: A Basic Guide to the Collection and Care of Common Insects for Children Connie Zakowski (Rainbow Books, 1997).

Insectlopedia Douglas Florian (Harcourt, 1998).

Insects L. A. Mound (Dorling Kindersley, 2003).

Insects and Spiders Edward Parker (Raintree Steck-Vaughn, 2003).

The Life Cycle of Insects Louise and Richard Spilsbury (Heinemann Library, 2003).

National Audubon Society Field Guide to North American Insects and Spiders Lorus and Margery Milne (Knopf, 2003).

Mammals

Animal Habitats Tony Hare (Checkmark, 2001) and **Animal Life Cycles** (2001).

Grzimek's Encyclopedia of Mammals (5 volumes) Bernhard Grzimek (McGraw-Hill, 1990).

A Guide to Animal Tracking and Behavior Donald W. and Lillian Q. Stokes (Little, Brown, and Company, 1986).

Mammal Steve Parker (Dorling Kindersley, 2000).

National Audubon Society Field Guide to North American Mammals John O. Whitaker (Knopf, 1996).

National Audubon Society Guide to Marine Mammals of the World Randall R. Reeves and others (Knopf, 2002).

The Sierra Club Book of Great Mammals Linsay Knight (Sierra Club, 1992).

Rocks & Minerals

Earth Treasures: Where to Collect Minerals, Rocks & Fossils in the United States (4 volumes) Allan W. Eckert (Perennial Library, Harper & Row, 1987).

A Field Guide to Rocks and Minerals Frederick H. Pough (Houghton Mifflin, 1996) and **The Peterson First Guide to Rocks and Minerals** (1991).

Handbook of Rocks, Minerals and Gemstones Walter Schumann (Houghton Mifflin, 1993).

Mineralogy for Amateurs John Sinkankas (Van Nostrand, 1964).

National Audubon Society Field Guide to North American Rocks and Minerals Charles W. Chesterman (Knopf, 1978).

National Audubon Society First Field Guides: Rocks and Minerals Edward R. Riccuiti and Margaret W. Carruthers (Scholastic, 1998).

Sea Shells

American Seashells R. Tucker Abbott (Van Nostrand, 1974) and *Seashells of North America* (St. Martin's, 1996).

The Edge of the Sea Rachel Carson (Houghton Mifflin, 1955).

The Encyclopedia of Shells Kenneth R. Wye (Chartwell, 2000).

A Natural History of Shells Geerat J. Vermeij (Princeton, 1993).

Shells S. Peter Dance (Dorling Kindersley, 2002).

Trees

America's Forests Frank J. Staub (Carolrhoda, 1999).

The Audubon Society Field Guide to North American Trees (2 volumes) Elbert L. Little (Knopf, 1980).

Encyclopedia of North American Trees Sam Benvie (Firefly Books, 2000).

The Illustrated Encyclopedia of Trees David More and John White (Timber Press, 2002).

North American Landscape Trees Arthur L. Jacobson (Ten Speed, 1996).

Science Project Ideas About Trees Robert Gardner (Enslow, 1997).

Trees: Their Natural History Peter Thomas (Cambridge, 2000).

Trees of North America C. Frank Brockman (St. Martin's, 2001).

Trees of the Northern United States and Canada John L. Farrar (Iowa State University Press, 1995).

Wild Flowers

A Field Guide to Medicinal Plants and Herbs of Eastern and Central North America Steven Foster and J. A. Duke (Houghton Mifflin, 2000).

A Field Guide to Western Medicinal Plants and Herbs Steven Foster and Christopher Hobbs (Houghton Mifflin, 2002).

National Audubon Society Field Guide to North American Wildflowers: Eastern Region John W. Thieret and others (Knopf, 2001).

National Audubon Society Field Guide to North American Wildflowers: Western Region Richard Spellenberg (Knopf, 2001).

The Nature and Science of Flowers Jane Burton and Kim Taylor (Gareth Stevens, 1998).

Wildflowers (National Geographic Society, 2002).

Wildflowers of North America Frank D. Venning (Golden Press, 1984).

Places to Visit

To learn more about the subjects covered in *World Book's Science & Nature Guides* series, try to visit some of these interesting places. You can find more places to visit by checking with your teacher and with libraries, museums, and wildlife refuges. The Internet also has sites that describe interesting destinations.

Amphibians & Reptiles

Back Bay National Wildlife Refuge in Virginia Beach, Virginia, has tidal marshes, freshwater ponds, and brackish (slightly salty) ponds that give homes to snapping turtles, mud turtles, and other species.

At **Big Bend National Park** in Texas, more than 800,000 acres (325 hectares) of Chihuahuan Desert are home to horned lizards, rattlesnakes, geckos, and many other desert species.

Corkscrew Swamp Sanctuary in Naples, Florida, features a boardwalk through cypress swamps, where you may see tree lizards, American alligators, and a wide variety of snakes.

Everglades National Park in southern Florida is a "river of grass" that is home to water snakes (such as cottonmouths), American alligators, softshell turtles, and many amphibians.

Exotarium Ferme de Reptiles, Saint-Eustache, Quebec, Canada, houses more than 300 snakes, crocodiles, lizards, frogs, and other cold-blooded animals.

Great Smoky Mountains National Park, on the border of Tennessee and North Carolina, is home to numerous species of salamanders—North America's largest collection. The moist forests shelter more than 80 species of amphibians and reptiles.

Wind Cave National Park in Hot Springs, South Dakota, is best known for its cave system. This is also an area where grasslands and Rocky Mountain forests meet. Look for such species as the Great Plains toad, western hognose snake, yellow-bellied racer, and western rattlesnake.

Birds

Acadia National Park, on the coast of Maine, contains over 47,000 acres (19 hectares) of mountains, woodlands, lakes and ponds, and ocean shoreline, giving the park great diversity of habitat for birds.

Cape May National Wildlife Refuge, on the Delaware Bay in southern New Jersey, provides habitat to a wide variety of migratory birds.

Chincoteague National Wildlife Refuge has some 14,000 acres (6 hectares) of beaches, dunes, and marshes in which to observe birds. Most of the refuge is located in Virginia on Assateague Island.

Chiricahua Mountains in southeastern Arizona allows birders to see birds found nowhere else in the United States in an unusual setting of volcanic formations.

Corkscrew Swamp Sanctuary in northern Florida and **Everglades National Park** in southern Florida both feature a large number of bird species.

For hawk watching, both the **Holiday Beach Migration Observatory** in Malden Center, or the **Hawk Cliff Foundation** in Port Stanley, both in Ontario, Canada, are good choices.

Alberta's **Inglewood Bird Sanctuary** in Calgary, Canada, is visited by over 250 migrant bird species.

Jamaica Bay Wildlife Refuge, in Brooklyn and Queens (boroughs of New York City, New York), is an important urban wildlife refuge with diverse habitats.

Klamath Basin wildlife refuges in southern Oregon and northern California feature many types of birds in diverse habitats.

Padre Island National Seashore, off Corpus Christi, Texas, is the longest remaining undeveloped stretch of barrier island in the world and has a large number of birds.

Upper Souris National Wildlife Refuge, in northwestern North Dakota, is one of several national wildlife refuges in the waterfowl migration corridor know as the Central Flyway. **Horicon**

National Wildlife Refuge in southeastern Wisconsin is one of the largest freshwater wetlands in the Midwest and also forms part of this flyway.

Butterflies

Jutting far into Delaware Bay, **Cape May,** in New Jersey, is a major gathering point for migrating monarchs from late August to early October. Painted ladies, buckeyes, sulfurs, and many other butterflies can also be spotted here.

The **Fletcher Wildlife Garden** in Ontario, Canada, hosts more than 30 species of butterflies that inhabit the woodland areas of eastern Canada.

Tropical butterflies can be found in the few remaining undisturbed islands of the keys in Florida. Two of the best places are **Key Deer National Wildlife Refuge** and **Biscayne National Park.**

Natural Bridges State Park in Santa Cruz is the largest of several wintering sites for monarchs in southern California.

Rocky Mountain National Park in Estes Park, Colorado, has a variety of mountainous habitats, including high meadows, where such tundra butterfly species as arctics and alpines can be seen.

Santa Ana National Wildlife Refuge, in Alamo, Texas, and several neighboring refuges—including **Laguna Atascosa National Wildlife Refuge**—preserve subtropical forests where butterflies abound. More than 300 species have been recorded here—the greatest number anywhere in the United States.

Fossils

The American Museum of Natural History in New York City has one of the greatest collections of fossilized animals and other organisms in the world.

Pennsylvania's anthracite fields, in the **Appalachian Mountains**, produce fine fossil seed ferns and other treasures of the Carboniferous Period (360 million to 286 million years ago).

Dinosaur fossils are common in the **Badlands** of Montana, the site of famous *Tyrannosaurus rex* and *Maiasaura* finds.

Tours visit the **Burgess Shale,** a rock formation in the Canadian Rockies, where rare types of Cambrian fossils have been found. The site is located in the Yoho National Park in British Columbia, and no private collecting is permitted.

A wide variety of fossils are on display at the **Carnegie Museum of Natural History** in Pittsburgh, Pennsylvania.

Dinosaur Provincial Park in the badlands of the Red Deer River region in southern Alberta, Canada, hosts a working research site, where scientists from the Royal Tyrrell Museum search for dinosaur fossils each summer.

The **Dinosaur Quarry Visitor Center,** at Dinosaur National Monument in Jensen, Utah, is a working research site open to the public. It has many dramatic skeletal remains on view.

The Field Museum in Chicago, Illinois, has numerous fossil animals on display including Sue, the largest and most complete *Tyrannosaurus rex* ever found.

The **Green River** shales in southwestern Wyoming include perfectly preserved fossilized fish from the Tertiary Period (65 million to 2 million years ago).

Florida's **Itchtucknee River** is very rich in fossils. You can also find fossilized shark's teeth on beaches and mammal fossils from the Pleistocene Epoch (2 million to 11,500 years ago) on the state's east coast.

In north-central Oregon, the **John Day** fossil beds are noted for their mammal remains from the Tertiary Period (65 million to 2 million years ago).

Rich fossil beds in **Mazon Creek,** in northeastern Illinois, hold fossil plants, insects, and vertebrates from the Carboniferous Period (360 million to 206 million years ago).

Harvard's **Museum of Comparative Zoology** in Cambridge, Massachusetts, includes an extensive collection of fossils.

The Page Museum, at the site of the La Brea tar pits in Los Angeles, California, includes an excellent collection of mammal fossils from the Pleistocene Epoch (2 million to 11,500 years ago).

Visitors can marvel at an incredible variety of fossils at the **Smithsonian National Museum of Natural History** in Washington, D.C.

Freshwater Life

Back Bay National Wildlife Refuge in Virginia Beach, Virginia, has tidal marshes, freshwater ponds, and brackish (slightly salty) ponds—homes for snapping turtles, mud turtles, and other species.

Buffalo National River in Harrison, Arkansas, flows for over 130 miles (210 kilometers) through the Ozarks. The river holds smallmouth bass, various sunfish and darter species, and other cool-water fishes.

The **Canadian Museum of Nature,** Ottawa, Ontario, displays amphibians, fish, reptiles, and invertebrates from Canada and other areas of the world.

Corkscrew Swamp Sanctuary in Naples, Florida, features a boardwalk through cypress swamps, where you may see a variety of reptiles in a freshwater habitat.

Everglades National Park in southern Florida is the home of water snakes (such as water moccasins), American alligators, softshell turtles, and many amphibians.

Georgian Bay Islands National Park, Ontario, Canada, consists of a group of freshwater islands and shoals in the northeastern arm of Lake Huron. It has a greater variety of amphibians and reptiles than any other Canadian national park. Rare species such as the eastern massasauga rattlesnake inhabit the park.

Great Smoky Mountains National Park, on the border of Tennessee and North Carolina, is the home of numerous species of salamanders—North America's largest collection. The moist forests shelter a total of more than 80 species of amphibians and reptiles.

In Wyoming, at the **LeHardy Rapids** in Yellowstone National Park, June is the month in which the violent rapids on the Yellowstone River fill with cutthroat trout. The fish fight their way up the rapids to spawn in Yellowstone Lake.

The best time to see the fish of the Lake Ontario region is during the spawning season. Visit the **Salmon River Hatchery** at Altmar, New York. In spring and fall, the **Salmon River** near Pulaski, New York, fills with salmon and steelhead.

The Vancouver Aquarium, Vancouver, British Columbia, includes many freshwater as well as marine creatures, including fish, frogs, snakes, and spiders.

Insects

Big Cypress National Reserve in Ochopee, Florida, has a wide variety of habitats, including sawgrass, marshes, hardwood hummocks, and mangrove stands. It hosts many subtropical insects not found in the rest of the United States.

Black Kettle National Grassland in Cheyenne, Oklahoma, has large lakes surrounded by tallgrass prairie. There are many grassland species of butterflies, in addition to dragonflies and other insects.

The **Canadian Museum of Nature,** located in Ottawa, has an insect collection of more than 500,000 specimens. The **Canadian National Collection of Insects, Arachnids, and Nematodes,** also in Ottawa, has an estimated 16 million specimens, the majority of which are from Canada and the rest of North America.

Coronado National Forest on the border of Arizona and New Mexico features more than 1.7 million acres (.7 million hectares), ranging from desert to mountains, making this an ideal place to search for different kinds of southwestern insects.

Death Valley National Monument, in Death Valley, California, looks barren, but actually supports many forms of life, including desert insects.

North Cascades National Park in Sedro-Woolley is high in the Cascade Mountains in the state of Washington. This park has deep forests and mountain meadows full of wildflowers, which are excellent places to look for northern species of insects.

At **Shenandoah National Park** in Luray, Virginia, many insects typical of the Appalachian oak forests are common. If you see a large area of dead trees, the destruction is likely to be the work of gypsy moths, a pest imported from Europe.

Mammals

Baxter State Park in Millinocket, Maine, is a huge area of wilderness around Mount Katahdin. Baxter is home to deer, coyotes, black bears, lynx, snowshoe hares, fishers, and other mammals. Moose are often spotted there feeding in ponds and lakes.

Big Bend National Park, in the Chihuahuan Desert in Texas, holds many mammals, though most come out only at night and are hard to see. There are mountain lions, armadillos, kangaroo rats, black-tailed jack rabbits, peccaries, and mule deer.

Channel Islands National Park is a chain of islands off the southern California coast that attracts large numbers of harbor seals, California sea lions, and the gigantic elephant seals. During winter, gray whales feed in the waters around the islands.

On the border of Tennessee and North Carolina, white-tailed deer and black bears are common in the **Great Smoky Mountains National Park.** Smaller mammals in the park include chipmunks, foxes, woodchucks, raccoons, bats, and skunks.

Gros Morne National Park, Newfoundland and Labrador, Canada, has a varied landscape where more than 20 species of mammals—including a herd of caribou—roam freely.

National Bison Range in Moiese, Montana, is home to a large herd of wild bison. This refuge also holds deer, pronghorn antelope, elk, coyotes, and other mammals.

Yellowstone National Park in Wyoming is one of the best places for viewing Rocky Mountain mammals, including bears, elk, bison, moose, coyotes, and wolves.

Rocks & Minerals

Arizona may be one of the most mineralogically varied states of all, with such prizes as gold, silver, copper, and turquoise. There is also an abundance of petrified wood to be found.

California is geologically complex, with excellent collecting opportunities in San Bernadino and San Diego counties, among other locations.

In **Canada**, the western mountain ranges are good locations for finding many types of rocks and minerals. In southwestern British Columbia, deposits include agate, gold, jadeite, and quartz. In southeastern Ontario, near the town of Bancroft, weathering has exposed very old metamorphic and volcanic rock, including apatite, feldspars, fluorite, granite, marble, and deep blue sodalite.

In **New York,** the rock crystals known as "Herkimer Diamonds" are commonly found in Herkimer County, in the Adirondack Mountains.

North Carolina has an exceptional store of rocks and minerals, especially in the Appalachians of the western part of the state.

The Pacific coast beaches of **Oregon** produce such wave-tossed mineral specimens as agate, jasper, and moonstones. Obsidian is the main attraction at Glass Butte, near Pineville.

The anthracite fields of **Pennsylvania** produce not only hard coal, but also plentiful fossils from the

Carboniferous Period (360 million to 286 million years ago). The state's southeastern region is famous for garnets, moonstones, and amethyst.

Collectors flock to the central valleys of **Vermont** for rare forms of serpentine.

Washington, like Oregon, is a good place to find agate, jasper, and other minerals along the beaches of the Pacific coast.

Sea Shells

The beaches of **Assateague Island National Seashore** (including **Chincoteague National Wildlife Refuge**) in Maryland and Virginia are excellent places for shell collecting.

The sand beaches of **Cape Cod,** in Massachusetts, offer some of the best shelling on the East Coast. Cape Cod forms a natural boundary—it's the most southerly point for many cold-water species and the most northerly point for many southern shells.

Fundy National Park, New Brunswick, Canada, includes the Bay of Fundy, which has some of the world's strongest tides. Millions of shells wash up and you can see them at low tide.

Hidden Beach and other coastal areas in **Redwood National Park** in northern California are well worth a visit by serious shell collectors.

The coastal areas of **Olympic National Park** in Washington state offer scallops and other shells to collectors. Many visitors also enjoy the park's famous tide pools, where live shellfish can be found.

Many shell collectors come to the **Outer Banks** of North Carolina to look for new and unusual specimens.

Pacific Rim National Park Reserve, British Columbia, Canada, is an intertidal habitat for many mollusks. Sea shells can be found in its tidepools and along the beach, but collecting them is prohibited.

Florida is one of the best shell-collecting regions in North America, with its gentle sand beaches and diverse selection of subtropical species. Almost any

beach will do, but **Sanibel** and **Captiva** islands, off the coast in the Gulf of Mexico, have the most famous beaches for shelling. Sanibel also has a shell museum that displays unusual specimens.

Yaquina Head Natural Area, on Oregon's northern coast, features smooth beaches and tide pools where a variety of shells and shellfish can be found.

Trees

Adirondack Forest Preserve in New York is a fine hardwood forest.

Banff National Park in Alberta, Canada, has beautiful, huge pine forests in the Canadian Rockies.

Subtropical forest in the United States is restricted to Florida; the best place to see it is in **Everglades National Park.** Ancient baldcypress forests can be found at **Corkscrew Swamp Sanctuary.**

Fundy National Park in Alma, New Brunswick, features conifer-dominated forests on the Bay of Fundy in Canada.

Great Smoky Mountains National Park on the border between Tennessee and North Carolina includes exceptional hardwoods.

Green Mountain National Forest in Vermont has large areas of hardwoods, as well.

Joyce Kilmer Memorial Forest, part of Nantahala National Forest, preserves one of the largest tracts of virgin hardwoods remaining in the eastern United States.

The Pine Barrens in New Jersey feature some of the most unusual forest communities in North America.

North America's largest trees are in California. Giant sequoias grow tall in **Sequoia National Park.** Towering coastal redwoods are found in **Redwoods National Park** and **Muir Woods National Monument.**

In **Washington state,** temperate rain forest with huge Sitka spruce and western redcedar can be seen in **Olympic National Park** and **Olympic National Forest.**

Wild Flowers

Adirondack Forest Preserve in New York has many beautiful eastern wild flowers for visitors to enjoy.

Bartholomew's Cobble in Massachusetts boasts one of the most all-inclusive wild flower communities in the United States.

Bruce Peninsula National Park, Ontario, Canada, boasts more than 40 species of wild orchids, plus many other kinds of wild flowers.

Perhaps no wild flower spectacle in the West matches the bloom of California wild poppies at **California State Antelope Valley Poppy Reserve,** where the land usually turns orange to the horizon from March through May.

Cranberry Glades Botanical Area in Monongahela National Forest in West Virginia has various bog plants, including orchids, that bloom in midsummer.

Crater Lake National Park in Oregon offers wonderful opportunities to see western wild flowers.

Curlew Prairie in Iowa is a fine remnant prairie with native midwestern wild flowers.

Great Smoky Mountains National Park in Tennessee features mountainous habitats with various eastern wild flowers.

Hoosier Prairie Nature Reserve in Indiana is enjoyed by many wild flower lovers, especially during the summer blooms.

Konza Prairie and **Flint Hills Tallgrass Prairie** in Kansas feature large areas of remnant prairie that bursts into flower during summer.

In Arizona, a wet winter may produce astonishing blooms from normally dry land from February to April in **Organ Pipe Cactus National Monument.** This is a great place to see cactus flowers.

Pawnee Prairie and **Valentine National Wildlife Preserve** in Nebraska offer spectacular examples of North American prairie wild flowers.

To see western forest wild flowers, plan a visit to **Rocky Mountain National Park** in Colorado.

Shenandoah National Park in Virginia offers excellent examples of wild flowers in eastern forests.

Shenk's Ferry Glen Wildflower Preserve and **Enlow Fork Natural Area** in Pennsylvania have superb collections of eastern wild flowers.

Yellowstone National Park in Wyoming is one of the best places to see western wild flowers.

Organizations

The following groups offer more information about the subjects covered in the individual field guides in *World Book's Science & Nature Guides* series. There are many other organizations in addition to these, which you can find out about from your teacher, your local library, or Internet sources.

Here are some general organizations that pertain to many subjects in the series.

Many of the preserves owned by the **Nature Conservancy** and its chapters conserve unique and threatened habitats. The conservancy is one of the best sources for information about plants and animals in the United States. Contact: Nature Conservancy, Suite 100, 4245 North Fairfax Drive, Arlington, Virginia 22203-1606; (800) 628-6860. http://nature.org

For information about national parks, contact: **National Park Service,** 1849 C Street NW, Washington, D.C. 20240; (202) 208-6843. http://www.nps.gov

For a complete listing of **National Wildlife Refuges** in the United States, contact: National Wildlife Refuge System, U.S. Fish & Wildlife Service; (800) 344-WILD. http://refuges.fws.gov

In Canada, the **Canadian Nature Federation** is a good starting point. Contact: Canadian Nature Federation, Suite 606, 1 Nicholas Street, Ottawa, Ontario K1N 787; (800) 267-4088. http://www.cnf.ca

Amphibians & Reptiles

The **American Society of Ichthyologists and Herpetologists** is a group for professional zoologists and serious amateurs. (Ichthyology is the study of fish; herpetology is the study of reptiles.) Contact: The American Society of Ichthyologists and Herpetologists, Department of Biological Sciences, Florida International University, North Miami, Florida 33181; (305) 919-5651. http://www.asih.org

Students and scientists can contact the **Herpetologist League.** Contact: Herpetologist League, P.O. Box 519, Bainbridge, Georgia 39818; (229) 246-7374. http://www.inhs.uiuc.edu/cbd/cbd/HL/HL.html

On the East Coast, you should contact the **New England Herpetological Society.** Contact: New England Herpetological Society, P.O. Box 81, Somerville, Massachusetts 02143; (617) 789-5800. http://www.neherp.com

Society for the Study of Amphibians and Reptiles is a good group to contact. Contact: Society for the Study of Amphibians and Reptiles, P.O. Box 253, Marceline, Missouri 64658-0253; (660) 256-3252. http://www.ssarherps.org

Birds

The **American Birding Association** is the largest all-birding organization in North America, and publishes a bimonthly magazine, *Birding*, along with a monthly newsletter, *Winging It*. Contact: American Birding Association, Box 6599, Colorado Springs, Colorado 80934; (719) 578-9703. http://www.americanbirding.org

The world-famous **Cornell Lab of Ornithology** accepts associate members and allows them the chance to take part in a number of cooperative research ventures, including Project Feeder Watch. Members also receive the lab's quarterly magazine, *Living Bird*. Contact: Cornell Lab of Ornithology, 159 Sapsucker Woods Road, Ithaca, New York 14850; (800) 843-2473. http://www.birds.cornell.edu

The **National Audubon Society** is most often associated with birds, but in recent years it has become more involved in general environmental issues. Contact: National Audubon Society, 700 Broadway, New York, New York 10003; (212) 979-3000. http://www.audubon.org

There are also affiliated and independent Audubon Societies in every state.

Butterflies

The **North American Butterfly Association** publishes a quarterly magazine, *American Butterflies,* and seeks to promote butterfly watching. Contact: North American Butterfly Association, 4 Delaware Road, Morristown, New Jersey 07960. http://www.naba.org

The **Northern Prairie Wildlife Research Center,** part of the U.S. Department of the Interior's Geological Survey, has a very useful Web site for butterfly watchers in the United States: http://www.npwrc.usgs.gov/resource/distr/lepid/bfl yusa/bflyusa.htm

The **Xerces Society** is a national society for invertebrate (animals without backbones) enthusiasts. Contact: Xerces Society, 4828 SE Hawthorne Boulevard, Portland, Oregon 97215; (503) 232-6639. http://www.xerces.org

The **Young Entomologist's Society** publishes *Insect World,* a magazine containing articles about insects that are of interest to the beginner. Write to: Young Entomologist's Society, 6907 West Grand River Avenue, Lansing, Michigan 48906-9131. http://members.aol.com/YESbugs/mainmenu.html

Fossils

The **American Federation of Mineralogical Societies** is a hobby- and education-oriented group dedicated to the study and appreciation of earth sciences, including fossil hunting. It publishes the *A.F.M.S. Newsletter.* Contact: American Federation of Mineralogical Societies, 2706 Lascassas Pike, Murfreesboro, Tennessee 37130-1540; (615) 893-8270. http://www.amfed.org

The **American Paleontological Society** is at the forefront of organizations promoting fossil hunting and paleontology. http://www.paleosoc.org

In Canada, **Geological Survey of Canada** is the best source. Contact: the Geological Survey of Canada, Natural Resources, Canada, Earth Sciences Sector, 601 Booth St., Ottawa, Ontario K1A 0E8; (613) 996-3919. http://www.nrcan.gc.ca/gsc/index_e.html

The **U.S. Geological Survey** is one of the best sources of information about fossils and fossil-bearing deposits in the United States. For information, contact: Earth Science Information Center, 12201 Sunrise Valley Drive, Reston, Virginia 20192; (888) 275-8747. http://www.usgs.gov

Freshwater Life

The **American Society of Ichthyologists and Herpetologists** is a group for professional zoologists and serious amateurs. (Ichthyology is the study of fish; herpetology is the study of reptiles.) Contact: The American Society of Ichthyologists and Herpetologists, Department of Biological Sciences, Florida International University, North Miami, Florida 33181; (305) 919-5651. http://www.asih.org

North American Native Fishes Association is interested in studying and conserving American fish. Write to: North American Native Fishes Association, 1107 Argonne Drive, Baltimore, Maryland 21218. http://www.nanfa.org

Society for the Study of Amphibians and Reptiles is a good group for you to contact. Contact: Society for the Study of Amphibians and Reptiles, P.O. Box 253, Marceline, Missouri 64658-0253; (660) 256-3252. http://www.ssarherps.org

Insects

The **American Entomological Society** is for professionals and serious amateurs. It publishes *Entomological News.* Contact: American Entomological Society, Academy of Natural

Sciences of Philadelphia, 1900 Benjamin Franklin Parkway, Philadelphia, Pennsylvania 19103-1028; (215) 561-3978.
http://www.acnatsci.org/hosted/aes/index.html

The Dragonfly Society of the Americas focuses on these spectacular insects. Write to: The Dragonfly Society of the Americas, 2067 Little River Lane, Tallahassee, Florida 32311.
http://www.afn.org/~iori/dsaintro.html

The Lepidopterist's Society publishes a journal and a newsletter. Write to: The Lepidopterist's Society, 9417 Carvalho Court, Bakersfield, California 93311-1846.
http://alpha.furman.edu/~snyder/snyder/lep/index1.htm

The **Xerces Society** is a national society for invertebrate (animals without backbones) enthusiasts. Contact: Xerces Society, 4828 SE Hawthorne Boulevard, Portland, Oregon 97215; (503) 232-6639.
http://www.xerces.org

The **Young Entomologist's Society** publishes a magazine containing articles about insects that are of interest to the beginner. Write to: Young Entomologist's Society, 6907 West Grand River Avenue, Lansing, Michigan 48906-9131.
http://members.aol.com/YESbugs/mainmenu.html

Mammals

The **American Cetacean Society** is the best group to contact if you are interested in whales and dolphins. Contact: American Cetacean Society, P.O. Box 1391, San Pedro, California 90733-1391; (310) 548-6279.
http://www.acsonline.org

The **American Society of Mammalogists** accepts professional zoologists and serious amateurs as members. Write to: *Journal of Mammalogy*, Allen Marketing & Management, 810 East 10th Street, P.O. Box 1897, Lawrence, Kansas 66044-8897.
http://www.mammalsociety.org

Bat Conservation International is interested in everything to do with bats and their preservation. Contact: Bat Conservation International, P.O. Box 162603, Austin, Texas 78716-2603; (512) 327-9721.
http://www.batcon.org

If you are interested in wolves and in their conservation, contact the **Wolf Fund**. Write to: Wolf Fund, P.O. Box 471, Moose, Wyoming 83012.

Rocks & Minerals

The **American Federation of Mineralogical Societies** is a hobby- and education-oriented group dedicated to the study and appreciation of earth science; it publishes the *AFMS Newsletter*. Contact: American Federation of Mineralogical Societies, 2706 Lascassas Pike, Murfreesboro, Tennessee 37130-1540; (615) 893-8270.
http://www.amfed.org

The **Geological Society of America** is aimed primarily toward professional and academic geologists, but it can be a helpful contact for amateurs as well. Contact: Geological Society of America, P.O. Box 9140, Boulder, Colorado 80301-9140; (303) 447-2020.
http://www.geosociety.org

In Canada, the **Geological Survey of Canada** is the best starting point. Contact: Geological Survey of Canada, National Resources Canada, Earth Sciences Section, 601 Booth Street, Ottawa, Ontario K1A OE8; (613) 996-3919.
http://www.nrcan.gc.ca/gsc

The **Mineralogical Society of America** is aimed primarily toward professional and academic geologists. Contact: Mineralogical Society of America, Suite 601, 1015 Eighteenth St., NW, Washington, D.C. 20036-5212; (202) 775-4344.
http://www.minsocam.org

The **U.S. Geological Survey** is a terrific storehouse of information, including maps and guides. For additional information, contact: Earth Science Information Center, 12201 Sunrise Valley Drive, Reston, Virginia 20192; (888) 275-8747.
http://www.usgs.gov or http://ask.usgs.gov

Sea Shells

The **American Malacological Society** is an organization of professionals and hobbyists that publishes the *American Malacological Bulletin*. Write to: American Malacological Society, 4201 Wilson Blvd., Suite 110-455, Arlington, Virginia 22203-1859.
http://erato.acnatsci.org/ams

The **Conchologists of America** is a collector-oriented society promoting shellfish conservation and environmentally sound collecting practices. It publishes the quarterly *American Conchologist*. Write to: Conchologists of America, 1222 Holsworth Lane, Louisville, Kentucky 40222.
http://coa.acnatsci.org/conchnet

For Pacific Coast sea shell enthusiasts, there is the **Western Society of Malacologists,** open to professionals and amateurs. Write to: Western Society of Malacologists, P.O. Box 1995, Newport, Oregon 97365.
http://biology.fullerton.edu/wsm/index.html

Trees

American Forests' objective is proper management of forest lands; the group publishes *American Forests* magazine. Contact: American Forests, P.O. Box 2000, Washington, D.C. 20013; (202) 955–4500.
http://www.americanforests.org

In Canada, the **Canadian Forest Service** is the best starting point. Write to: Canadian Forest Service, Natural Resources Canada, 580 Booth Street, 8th Floor, Ottawa, Ontario K1A 0E4.
http://www.nrcan.gc.ca/cfs-scf/index_e.html

The **National Arbor Day Foundation** is dedicated to the planting and preservation of trees, from street trees to tropical forests. Write to: National Arbor Day Foundation, 100 Arbor Avenue, Nebraska City, Nebraska 68410.
http://www.arborday.org

For information about U.S. national forests, contact: **United States Department of Agriculture, Forest Service,** 1400 Independence Avenue SW, Washington, D.C. 20250-0002; (202) 205-8333.
http://www.fs.fed.us

Wild Flowers

The **American Association of Botanical Gardens and Arboreta** is the best source of information about botanical gardens. While not wild habitats, botanical gardens provide an excellent opportunity to see rare species of wild flowers and other plants. Contact: American Association of Botanical Gardens and Arboreta, 100 W. 10th Street, Suite 614, Wilmington, Delaware 19801; (302) 655-7100.
http://www.aabga.org

The **Lady Bird Johnson Wildflower Center** is one of the best beginning points for wild flower buffs. The center publishes a variety of material with information on wild flowers and related organizations throughout North America. Contact: Lady Bird Johnson Wildflower Center, 4801 La Crosse Avenue, Austin, Texas 78739; (512) 292-4100.
http://www.wildflower.org

The **North American Native Plant Society** publishes one of North America's foremost native plant magazines, *Wildflower*. Write to: North American Native Plant Society, P.O. Box 84, Station D, Etobicoke, Ontario M9A 4X1.
http://www.nanps.org/index.shtml

Glossary

A

abdomen: in insects, the third section of the body, which carries the ovipositor

acid: chemical compound with a sour taste; acid turns blue litmus paper red

adaptation: change made by organisms to better fit new conditions

aggregate: rock made from a mixture of mineral fragments

alpine meadow: high meadow found on mountains above the timberline

amber: hard, yellowish-brown fossilized resin that comes chiefly from pine trees millions of years old; it sometimes contains preserved remains of organisms

ammonite: extinct mollusk with a spiral-shaped shell

amorphous: in rocks and minerals, a crystal lacking a particular pattern or regular structure

amphibian: cold-blooded animal that was the first vertebrate (animal with a backbone) to spend part of its life on land (unlike fish, which spend all their lives underwater); amphibians lay their eggs in water and the young start life there, breathing through gills; amphibians then usually develop into an adult form, using lungs to breathe, and living on land

annual: a plant that dies after one year

anther: in flowers, one of the knobs at the top of the stamens that contain pollen

aperture: in mollusks, the main opening of a gastropod shell

apex: in mollusks, the point of the spire on a gastropod shell

arthropod: large group of animals with jointed legs, such as insects, spiders, and lobsters

atom: basic unit of a chemical element

B

baleen plates: structures that some whales have that allow them to strain the water for tiny shrimps and plankton

barbel: "whisker" on the chins of certain fish, including members of the catfish family

batholith: in rocks and minerals, a huge underground mass of solidified igneous rock

bayou: slow-running, marshy inlet or outflow of a lake or river

beak: in mollusks, the first part of a bivalve's shells to form; just above the hinge

bib: area of a bird's body under its beak

biennial: plant that dies after two years

bivalve: mollusk with two shells, or valves, hinged together, such as a clam or oyster

bog: soft, wet, spongy ground; marsh

bract: in flowering plants, a modified and often scalelike leaf found at the base of a flower or fruit

broadleaf tree: tree with broad, flat leaves that usually drop off in the fall

brood: group of young birds hatched at the same time in a nest and cared for together

bulb: in plants, a thick, roundish underground structure that stores food

byssus: in mollusks, a clump of "threads" used by certain species to anchor themselves to rocks

C

calcium carbonate: limestone

call: short sounds that a bird, or certain other animals, makes

camouflage: in animals, coloration or other disguise that allows an animal to blend with its environment

canal: in mollusks, the channel at the lower end of a gastropod shell through which the siphon is extended

canopy: extent of the branches of a tree

cap: area around the top of a bird's head; larger than the crown

carapace: shell or bony covering on the back of some animals, such as lobsters and turtles

carbonate: crystallized compound that includes a solidified form of carbonic acid (CO_3)

carnivore: any animal that eats mostly meat

caterpillar: young stage of a butterfly or moth, when it looks very different from the adult

catkin: in flowers, a drooping cluster

cavity: hole in a rock mass, often lined with crystals

cheek: in birds, the area of the head just below the eye

chloride: salt crystallized from hydrochloric acid

chlorophyll: green substance in plants that takes in light energy for use in photosynthesis

chrysalis: inactive pupal stage in the development of a caterpillar into an adult butterfly

cleavage: in rocks and minerals, the line along which a crystal will easily break to form a flat surface

compound, chemical: a mixture of two or more chemical elements

compound leaf: in plants, one large leaf made of several small leaflets

conifer: large group of trees or shrubs that bears its seeds in cones

contrary: in mollusks, any gastropod shell coiled to the left

coprolite: fossilized excrement

cord, spiral: on a sea shell, one of the horizontal bands on a whorl

core: name for the center of Earth; made mostly of molten iron

corm: food-rich underground stem in plants

country rock: rock type underlying an area of the landscape

crest: in birds, the small tuft of feathers at the top of the head

crinkly: in plants, twisted leaves, as in the holly

crown: (1) area at the very top of a bird's head, smaller than the cap; (2) mass of branches and twigs at the top of a tree

crust: outer layer of Earth

crustacean: soft-bodied animal without a backbone; crustaceans have a hard outer shell, long feelers, and many pairs of jointed legs

crystal: in rocks and minerals, a naturally occurring mineral with many flat surfaces

crystal systems: in rocks and minerals, the various shapes of crystals

cubic. *See isometric*

cultivar: new type of plant variety produced by selective breeding

D

deciduous: tree that loses its leaves in the fall; most broadleaf trees are deciduous

deposit: in rocks and minerals, a vein, dike, or other mineral formation present in large quantities

desert: dry, barren area where only about half the ground has plant cover; found in the southwestern United States and in other areas

dike: in rocks and minerals, a thin sheet of igneous rock that forces its way as magma into a vertical crack in country rock

dimorphic: species in which the male and female don't look at all alike

E

ear: in mollusks, handlelike structures found on scallop shells on each side of the hinge

echolocation: using high-pitched sounds to locate food and avoid hitting things in the dark; bats use echolocation

ecosystem: interactions of plants and animals that form a living habitat

ectoparasite: harmful, parasitic organism that lives on the surface of an animal's body

eft: young stage of a salamander or newt

element, chemical: pure substance that contains only one kind of atom

endoparasite: harmful, parasitic organism that lives inside an animal's body

enzyme: a substance produced by the body to speed up chemical reactions—for example, to help digest food

erosion: wearing away of rocks by the action of wind or water

evaporation: process by which a liquid turns into a gas

evergreen: tree or shrub with needlelike or flat leaves that keeps its leaves throughout the year

evolution: theory describing the process by which plants, animals, or other organisms change over time

exoskeleton: hard outer case or shell of some invertebrates

eyespot: in insects such as butterflies, a brightly colored or dark marking on the wings that look like a large eye

F

feldspar: one of a group of rock-forming silicate minerals

fertile: refers to land that is rich in nutrients and other things that help plants grow

filter feeder: animal that lives in water and takes in small pieces of drifting material for food

fledgling: young bird just able to fly

floret: tiny disk or ray flower that is packed into a composite flower head (a flower head made of many tiny flowers)

forage: to hunt or search for food

forewing: one of the front pair of wings on an insect

fossil: remains or markings of a once-living plant or animal found within rock

fungi: organism that lacks chlorophyll, the green coloring matter that many plants use to make food

G

gall: abnormal growth on plants that is often seen as a rounded swelling; these are usually produced because of parasites such as gall wasps

gape: in mollusks, the opening between the two valves that remains when a bivalve is closed

gastropod: mollusk with a single shell, which may be either coiled or cap-shaped, such as a snail or conch

gem/gemstone: crystal that is cut and polished for display

geology: study of rocks and minerals

glade: small open space in a forest

gland: any of several small organs that control certain functions of the body; glands may produce milk, sweat, scent chemicals, or other substances

grafting: placing of a shoot or bud from one plant into a slit in another plant, so that the shoot will grow as part of the second plant

grain: in rocks and minerals, a very small fragment of a mineral

gymnosperm: plant in which the seeds are not enclosed in fruit

H

habitat: environment (area) that is the natural home of certain animals and plants

herbivore: any animal that eats mostly plants

hermaphrodite: animal with both male and female sex organs

hexagonal: in rocks and minerals, one of the crystal systems

hibernate: to live in a deep sleep through winter

hindwing: in insects, one of the back pairs of wings

hinge: in mollusks, the pivoting point from which a bivalve opens and closes

homing: ability of a bird or other animal to return home from a great distance

honeydew: sweet substance produced by aphids and other tiny insects

humus: dark brown, powdery soil that forms when plants and the bodies of insects and other animals decay

hybrid: especially in plants, offspring of parents of different breeds, varieties, or species

hydrate: mineral composed of silica and a metallic element, combined with water

hydrothermal veins: cracks in rock filled by new minerals that have formed from a solution of very hot water and existing minerals

I

igneous rock: rock formed from magma or lava when a volcano erupts

impurities: traces of various minerals in a substance

incubation: keeping eggs warm in order to hatch them

insectivore: animal, such as a shrew, that eats insects and other invertebrates

intertidal zone: area of the shore between the points of high and low tide

invertebrate: animal without an internal backbone

iridescent: displaying changing colors, like those of the rainbow

isometric: in rocks and minerals, one of the crystal systems

L

larva: early form of an insect, such as a caterpillar or grub, before it changes into an adult form

lava: molten (melted) or partly molten magma, when it emerges onto the earth's surface

leaflets: small leaves that are grouped together to form one large compound leaf, as in the ash tree

legumes: plants belonging to the pea or bean family

lichen: an organism that consists of an alga (simple plantlike organism) and a fungus living as a single unit

ligament: in mollusks, a horny muscle that holds the two valves of a bivalve together

litter: family of young animals born together

lobed: leaf that has deeply divided edges, as in the maple

M

magma: molten (melted) rock beneath the earth's surface

malacology: study of mollusks

mammal: warm-blooded animals that give birth to live young (rather than lay eggs); mammals produce milk to feed their young

mantle: (1) layer of very hot rock under the earth's crust and on which the plates carrying the continents and ocean floor float; (2) flaps on a mollusk's body used to attach the animal to its shell

mask: band of color that runs across a bird's eyes

mass: in geology, a shapeless lump of rock or mineral

metamorphic rock: rock that has been altered by great heat and pressure or chemical activity

metamorphosis: in animals, extreme changes in form and appearance that occur in insects and certain other invertebrates while growing to maturity

mica: one of a group of minerals that splits in one direction into sheets. If hit with a sharp point, mica produces a six-pointed star around the point of impact

microhabitat: small area, such as a compost heap or window box, in which an animal lives

migration: journey from one part of the world to another, usually made in both spring and fall by certain birds

mollusk: soft-bodied animal without a backbone; most mollusks, such as snails and clams, have shells

molybdate: salt crystallized from an acid and containing molybdenum, or Mo

monoclinic: in rocks and minerals, one of the crystal systems

N

native: species that originated in a particular place

native mineral: mineral made from only one element, such as gold (Au), silver (Ag), copper (Cu), platinum (Pt), or mercury (Hg)

naturalized: species that was originally from one area, but that now flourishes in another area

nectar: sugary liquid produced by flowering plants and eaten by insects

needle: leaf of a conifer

nodule: small, rounded lump of a mineral or rock, usually found within a different type of rock

nugget: lump of metal, such as gold, or Au

nymph: young stage of certain winged insects, such as grasshoppers; nymphs that live underwater, such as those of mayflies and dragonflies, are usually called naiads

O

omnivore: animal that eats plants and other animals

opaque: cannot be seen through; opposite of transparent

operculum: horny plate that some mollusks use to seal the entrance to their shells

ore: rock or mineral from which a metal or other mineral can be extracted in commercial quantities

ornithischian: a "bird-hipped" dinosaur with lower hipbones that sweep backwards, like those of a bird

orthorhombic: in rocks and minerals, one of the crystal systems

ovary: in flowers, the part of the stigma where the egg cells are produced

over-layer: soft, often hairy layer on the outside of a sea shell that protects the shell as it grows

ovipositor: egg-laying structure on the abdomen of an adult female insect; in some insects, it also acts as a sting

ovule: egg cell; in plants, it develops into the seed

owl pellet: waste matter, usually containing animal bones, that an owl regurgitates after it has eaten

oxide: crystallized compound of oxygen (O), with a metallic element

oxidized: something that has combined with oxygen (O)

P

pallial line: in mollusks, the scar on a bivalve, parallel to the longest side, where the mantle is attached to the shell

palmate: leaf that has lobes or leaflets all coming from one central point, like in the maple or horse chestnut

parent rock: igneous or sedimentary rock from which metamorphic rock is made

pegmatite: very coarse-grained type of igneous rock, often found as dikes

perennial: a plant that lives for several flowering seasons

petrification: type of fossilization in which a dead organism's body is slowly replaced with minerals

pheromone: chemical substance produced by insects and certain other animals that affects the behavior or development of other members of their species

phosphate: compound containing the phosphate group, which has one phosphorus and four oxygen atoms (PO_4)

photosynthesis: process by which plants use the energy of sunlight, together with water and carbon dioxide (CO_2), to make their own food

pinnate: leaf that has several lobes or leaflets arranged directly across from each other on the sides of a stem

placer: deposit of sand or gravel in or near a river; it may contain gold (Au), platinum (Pt), or other heavy minerals

plagioclase: in rocks and minerals, any one of a group of feldspars that contains both sodium (Na) and calcium (Ca)

plankton: tiny invertebrates that live in water; some whales feed on nothing else

plate, continental: one of the sections of crust and upper mantle that move about, carrying the continents

plumage: feathers of a bird

pollen: in flowers, a powdery substance from the anthers that fertilizes (unites with) the egg cells in the ovary of a flower

pollination: in flowers, pollen being carried (for example, by wind or insects) from the anthers to the stigma

prairie: grasslands of central North America, stretching from the Appalachians to the Rockies

precious metal: gold (Au), silver (Ag), platinum (Pt), or some other rare metal

predator: carnivorous animal that eats other animals

proboscis: tubular, sucking mouthpiece of certain insects

pupa: (plural, pupae) inactive stage of an insect when it changes from a wingless larva to a winged adult

pyroxene: one of a group of silicate minerals containing groups of two silicon and six oxygen atoms (Si_2O_6)

Glossary

Q

quartz: common group of rock-forming silicate minerals

queen: a fully developed female in a colony of insects, such as bees or ants, that lays eggs

R

radula: in mollusks, a ribbon of flesh that bears rows of teeth

reptile: cold-blooded animal with a backbone; unlike amphibians, reptiles can spend all their lives on land, though some live in water

resin: sticky yellow or brown substance that flows from certain trees and other plants

rhizome: underground stem that can produce leaves and flowers that rise above the surface; it can also store food in some plants

rhombohedral: in rocks and minerals, one of the crystal systems

ribs, axial: in mollusks, vertical ridges on a whorl of a shell

ribs, radial: in mollusks, ridges running from a central point on a shell

roost: for a bird or bat, to sleep, or a sleeping or hibernating place

rosette: circular needle formation, as in larches

rostrum: beaklike extension at the front of the head of some insects, such as weevils

S

sap: sticky liquid that a tree uses to carry food to and from its roots and leaves

sapling: young tree

saurischian: "lizard-hipped" dinosaur with lower hipbones that fan out where the legs join the hips

savanna: grassland with a few trees and bushes and limited rainfall

scrub: large area of thicket with stunted trees, shrubs, and bushes growing thickly together

sculpture: relief patterns on a shell, such as cords, ribs, knobs, and spines

secondary growth: plant growth in semi-open country with scattered trees and thickets

secondary mineral: mineral changed by chemical reactions within its original rock

secretion: substance produced by a gland in the body, often containing enzymes

sedges: group of plants with rows of narrow, pointed leaves; usually found in marshy land

sediment: tiny piece of rock, weathered by wind or water, which makes up sedimentary rock

sedimentary rock: rock made from layer upon layer of mud, sand, and plant and animal remains, which have been compressed together deep underground, often under the sea

seed: fertilized egg (egg cell that has united with pollen) of a flower

sepal: green, leaflike part that protects a bud and grows around the base of the flower

sheet: in geology, a flat plate of a mineral that has formed horizontally between two layers of country rock

silicate: large group of minerals that always contain pyramid-shaped groupings of one silicon (Si) and four oxygen (O) atoms

sill: sheetlike body of igneous rock, typically lying horizontally between layers of country rock

siphon: tube that mollusks use to take in and expel water and food

solution: mixture of something dissolved in a liquid

song: long musical sounds that a bird makes, for purposes such as attracting a mate or establishing a territory

species: particular type of organism

specific gravity: test to identify a mineral

spire: in mollusks, all the whorls of a gastropod shell except the largest and lowest one, where the animal lives

stalactite: downward-growing column formed by dripping water containing a solution of limestone; may join with a stalagmite to make a pillar

stalagmite: upward-rising column of limestone, formed from the drip of a stalactite

stamens: male part of the flower; at the top of the stamens are the anthers

stigma: female part of the flower that contains the style and ovary

stomata: tiny holes in leaves that allow a plant to breathe. Carbon dioxide, oxygen, water vapor, and other gases pass into and out of the leaves through the stomata

strata: particular layers of sediments, squashed together into sedimentary rock

streak: in geology, the true color of a mineral, used for identification

style: tube in the stigma through which the pollen travels to the ovary

succulent: plant with thick, fleshy leaves or stems full of juice

sulfate: Minerals containing one or more metallic elements and groups of one sulfur and four oxygen atoms (SO_4)

sulfide: compound of sulfur (S) and one or more metallic elements—for example, arsenopyrite (FeAsS)

T

tadpole: young stage of a frog or toad

talon: claw of a bird of prey, such as an eagle or owl

tentacle: long, thin, fleshy finger on a mollusk's head for touching things

tetragonal: in rocks and minerals, one of the crystal systems

thicket: thick growth of scrub, underbrush, and small trees

thorax: middle section of an insect's body. It is divided into three segments, each of which carries a pair of legs. The back two segments also support the wings, if they exist.

thread: in mollusks, one of the fine spiral lines around the whorl of a shell

tooth: in mollusks, shelly ridge in the upper, hinged part of a valve

trace fossil: fossil that shows tracks, trails, burrows, or other signs of an ancient animal, rather than the remains of its body

tragus: flap of skin on a bat that protects the entrance to the ear; it also functions in echolocation

translucent: object which lets light through, but which is not able to be seen through clearly, such as frosted glass

transparent: describes something, such as plain glass, that can be seen through clearly

transpiration: process by which plants or other organisms release water vapor from a surface, such as from a leaf

triclinic: in rocks and minerals, one of the crystal systems

trigonal. *See rhombohedral*

trilobites: types of extinct sea-dwelling arthropods

tuber: thick part of an underground stem from which new plants can grow

tundra: vast, treeless region in cold regions of the world and on mountains

tungstate: minerals containing one or more metallic elements and groups of one tungsten and four oxygen atoms (WO_4)

tymbals: drumlike organs on either side of the thorax of a cicada; they vibrate to make the insect's song

U

ultra-basic: rock like the dolomites, containing little or no quartz or feldspars; made mainly of iron (Fe) and magnesium (Mg)

ungulate: type of mammal with hoofs and several stomach compartments, which help the animal digest plant material

V

valve: one of the two shells that make up a bivalve

variegated: leaves with more than one color

variety: mineral that has had another mineral or element mixed into it, producing a slightly different chemical result; example: a blue variety of pectolite called Larimar

vein: (1) vertical deposit of mineral that has seeped into a crack in country rock as a solution; (2) rib in a leaf

velvet: furry skin that covers a deer's antlers while they grow

vertebrate: animal with an internal backbone

viviparous: giving birth to live young, instead of laying eggs

W

wattle: fleshy, wrinkled piece of skin, often brightly colored, that hangs from the chin or throat of such birds as turkeys

wetland: area, such as a marsh or pond, that contains water during much or all of the year

whale: type of mammal that lives in the sea and never needs to come ashore

whorl: (1) one complete turn in a gastropod's shell; (2) group of leaves that grows at the same level around the stem

X

xylem: tiny tubes that carry water and food from the roots to the leaves of a plant

Z

zone fossil: fossil of a particular species that is used for dating rocks

Index

This index covers all 11 *Science & Nature Guides*. Each page number or group of page numbers is preceded by a boldface letter code for one of the *Guides*. For example:

alligator, **A:** 49, **Fr:** 6, 45

This means that there are references to alligators on page 49 of *Amphibians and Reptiles* and pages 6 and 45 of *Freshwater Life*. The complete list of letter codes follows.

A   *Amphibians and Reptiles*
Bi *Birds*
Bu *Butterflies*
Fo *Fossils*
Fr *Freshwater Life*
I   *Insects*
M   *Mammals*
R   *Rocks and Minerals*
S   *Sea Shells*
T   *Trees*
W   *Wild Flowers*

You will also find several index headings in which a code is used without page numbers following it, as in

butterfly, **Bu, I:** 5, 71

In this example, **Bu** used alone means that an entire *Guide* is devoted to butterflies. Besides this, there are many other references to this topic, including the two in *Insects* listed here.

A

abdomen, of butterfly, **Bu:** 6
Abert's towhee, **Bi:** 53
Acadian hairstreak, **Bu:** 25
Acadian province, **S:** 8
Acanthoscaphites, **Fo:** 44
Acer, **Fo:** 14
acid rain, **R:** 20, **T:** 70
acmon blue, **Bu:** 10
Aconcagua, **R:** 14
aconite, **W:** 38
acorn, **T:** 16
acorn woodpecker, **Bi:** 29
Acrocoelites, **Fo:** 46
Acrocyathus, **Fo:** 22
Acrolepis, **Fo:** 70
Actinoceras, **Fo:** 40
adder's-tongue, **W:** 35
adductor muscles, **S:** 7

admiral (butterfly), **Bu:** 6, 15, 75, **I:** 21
aesthete (cell), **S:** 49
African fire barb, **Fr:** 28
agate, **R:** 18, 69
aggregate, **R:** 34, 52, 55
agoseris, **W:** 34
ailanthus, **T:** 28, 29, 56
alabaster, **R:** 53
Alaska-cedar, **T:** 63
Alaska great-tellin, **S:** 55
albite, **R:** 70
alder, **T:** 10
alderfly, **Fr:** 4, **I:** 60
   larva, **Fr:** 38
Alethopteris, **Fo:** 12
Aleutian province, **S:** 42
alfalfa butterfly, **Bu:** 16
Alfalfa leafcutting bee, **I:** 18
algae, **Fo:** 15

Allegheny monkey flower, **W:** 50
alligator, **A:** 49, **Fr:** 6, 45
alligator lizard, **A:** 12
alligator snapping turtle, **Fr:** 48, 50
almandine, **R:** 72
alpine (butterfly), **Bu:** 22, 36
alpine checkered skipper, **Bu:** 35
aluminum, **R:** 30, 54–57, 61, 68, 70–75
Amaltheus, **Fo:** 43
amazonite, **R:** 55
amber, **Fo:** 9, **R:** 26
ambulacra, **Fo:** 24
American alligator, **A:** 49, **Fr:** 45
American apollo, **Bu:** 7, 27
American badger, **M:** 12
American beech, **T:** 11
American black bear, **M:** 53
American brookline, **W:** 51
American chestnut, **T:** 21
American cockroach, **I:** 10
American coot, **Bi:** 74
American copper, **Bu:** 48
American crocodile, **Fr:** 45
American crow, **Bi:** 14
American ear snail, **Fr:** 34
American eel, **Fr:** 15
American elk, **M:** 56
American elm, **T:** 12
American golden-plover, **Bi:** 54
American goldfinch, **Bi:** 46
American holly, **T:** 50
American hornbeam, **T:** 14
American horse mussel, **S:** 28
American kestrel, **Bi:** 43
American marten, **M:** 27, 61
American monarch butterfly, **I:** 33
American mountain ash, **T:** 45
American painted lady, **Bu:** 29

American pasqueflower, **W:** 26
American pika, **M:** 54
American pygmy shrew, **M:** 16
American redstart, **Bi:** 35
American robin, **Bi:** 8, 16
American shrew mole, **M:** 28
American speedwell, **W:** 51
American swallowtail, **Bu:** 7, 13
American toad, **A:** 10, **Fr:** 12
American wigeon, **Bi:** 70, 74
amethyst, **R:** 69
amethyst gem clam, **S:** 20
ammonite, **Fo:** 9, 40–45
ammonoid, **Fo:** 18
amphibian, **A, Fr:** 4, 6
   catching and handling, **A:** 2, 7, 15
   desert and scrub, **A:** 66, 68, 69
   forest and woodland, **A:** 16, 18–21, 23
   fossil, **Fo:** 4, 66, 74, 75
   found almost everywhere, **A:** 8–11, **Fr:** 12–13
   grassland, **A:** 56, 57
   handling, **Fr:** 19
   identifying, **A:** 6–7
   information sources, **A:** 78
   lake, marsh, and pond, **A:** 42–47, **Fr:** 24–27, 48, 49
   life cycle, **A:** 4, 30–31
   looking for, **A:** 14
   stream, river, and canal, **A:** 32–39, **Fr:** 58–61, 73
Amphiope, **Fo:** 27
amphissa, **S:** 47
amphiuma, **Fr:** 27
analcime, **R:** 46
Ancilla, **Fo:** 50
andalusite, **R:** 30, 70
andesine, **R:** 70
andesite, **R:** 11

Index

Index

Index

Index

Index